AMERYKA
100 YEARS OLD

A GLOBETROTTER'S VIEW

By

SYGURD WIŚNIOWSKI

Translated, Edited, and Arranged by

MARION MOORE COLEMAN

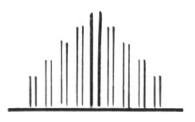

CHERRY HILL BOOKS — ISBN-0-910366
202 HIGHLAND AVE.   CHESHIRE, CONN. 06410
1972

Copyright © 1972 by A. P. and M. M. Coleman

Library of Congress Catalogue Card
Number 78-186272

International Standard Book Number O-910366-12-8

INTRODUCTION

FROM THE MARITSA TO THE MISSISSIPPI AND THE MISSOURI

It was along the River Maritsa, in what was then Rumelia and is now Bulgaria, that Sygurd Wiśniowski had his first foreign adventures. Born in Paniowce Zielone on the Galician side of the River Zbrucz, in 1841, when but seventeen he ran away from home, to take a job with a gang of fellow-countrymen who were being hired by the British government to put up a telegraph line across Turkey. In charge of the work was the Polish engineer Franciszek Sokulski, and there were many other Poles in the company beside Wiśniowski, notably the poet and future West Asian specialist, Karol Brzozowski, older than our hero by some sixteen years.

Many years later, in far off Minnesota, when travelling on a newly constructed and still totally unreliable railroad, Wiśniowski recalled an experience of those line-stringing days, and inserted it in his sketches of American life.[1] It seems that Brzozowski was the leader of the group to which Wiśniowski belonged, and responsible for getting out the work. They were approaching the River Maritsa and one of the linemen, whom Wiśniowski calls K, was trying to carry the line straight ahead, when a dense and seemingly impenetrable thicket blocked his way. When he asked Brzozowski how he was to manage against such a barrier, the leader of the company told him, "You want to get to the Maritsa? Well then, take a tent and two Bulgarians with axes, and let them start chopping. Drive them ahead of you and don't let them look back. Sooner or later you'll come to the Maritsa."

"But suppose they come upon a swamp along the way," K protested.

"Go around it in a semicircle. The English are giving the Turks enough money to pay for a few miles, more or less, extra."

So for four days K and his Bulgarians cut and hacked and wandered in the dense growth. Finally K saw daylight ahead and was sure he had reached the Maritsa at last. He tore through what remained of the thicket, though it almost put his eyes out, and there in the open field he saw Brzozowski, shooting red partridges.

"What are you doing here?" Brzozowski asked in surprise.

"Looking for the Maritsa," was K's shamefaced reply.

"And so, after hacking and chopping for four whole days, here you are, right back in our own camp," scolded the angry leader of our gang.

Everywhere he went, and nowhere more than in the United States, Wiśniowski found a story. Arriving here in the summer of 1873, he came with a quiver stuffed full of yarns, picked up in all the countries where he had stopped. In our country he yearned most of all to experience the Far West, still the romantic Never-Never Land, not merely of fiction but of reality, as he believed. And so, after a brief halt in Chicago, which, with its large Polish population, must have seemed but a transplanted Poland, he took off for a tour of Nebraska and Colorado. This was the most exciting period of his life, he was to write. Brief though it was, it provided him with more adventures than any before, and afforded him scenes "no artist could paint." He was profoundly impressed, for example, by the spectacle in Colorado of the Mount of the Holy Cross, with its vast, snow-white arms, outstretched across the background of the Rockies. Later he was to describe this, in *Langenor*, transposing the scene, however, to Montana.

Wherever he journeyed, on whatever continent, Wiśniowski was always obliged to alternate travel with periods of settled existence, in order to replenish his stock of cash. And so in the latter part of 1873 we find him settling down for a while in New Ulm, Minnesota, picking up a few pennies by writing for the local newspaper, the *New Ulm Herald*, sending accounts of his journeys to papers back home, and—of all things, farming! Outside New Ulm a little way he bought a piece of land which he proceeded to plant to wheat, following the example of the Germans and Scandinavians who had taken up much of the land in the region. In his spare moments he is said to have studied Chinese, with the idea in mind that five years of farming would give him enough money to visit the Far East, especially Central Asia. He also studied surveying, so as to have a skill which would bring him a living in whatever part of the Orient he might find himself.

For three years Wiśniowski remained on his farm, only to be driven out by grasshoppers, which seemed to harbor especial spite against his property. Later he was to use the grasshopper invasion in the novel *Langenor*, here translated, as well as in one of his *Sketches of American Life*, also included here.

In the summer of the very next year following his arrival in New Ulm, Wiśniowski had an historic, and for an adventurer like himself, enviable opportunity. In the role of correspondent for the *New Ulm Herald*, he accompanied the 7th United States Cavalry on its famous exploratory expedition into the Black Hills. Setting out from Fort Lincoln in North Dakota in July, 1874, General George Armstrong Custer led his troops into the formerly forbidding, and still Indian-controlled, land of the ponderosa pine. The purpose of the expedition was to determine whether rumors of gold in the Hills were well-founded, and to calm any fears the Sioux Indians might have that their hunting rights, guaranteed by treaty in 1868, would be violated.

The foray of 1874 was not the only experience Wiśniowski was to have of the Black Hills. The year following he joined a caravan bound for the west and again visited Custer City, as the gold camp was called, but what a change greeted his eyes! The hordes of miners who had poured into the place had devastated it, leaving but a single relatively quiet lodging house where a traveler could put up. Not content to end his journey here, Wiśniowski went on to Deadwood City, always seeking material for stories to be sent to the journals back home. The Custer expedition had given him "Lying Pete" as the hero of his tales, this excursion gave him Wild Jack, both of whom figure in the translations which follow in this book.

In the spring of 1874, when Wiśniowski had been in Minnesota less than a year, he was given the honorary, unpaid, job of Justice of the Peace. As a correspondent for the local paper, and by word of mouth, he had made himself known throughout the region by criticizing in the sharpest terms the do-nothing policy of local officials with respect to the farmers, who had lost everything from the grasshopper plague referred to above. Because of this, and thanks to his knowledge of German, politicians began to take notice of him and soon the Republican Party, which was in trouble in the New Ulm district, enlisted his services. First they made him a member of the committee organizing the local conventions that would choose delegates to the state convention. Wiśniowski went right to work for the party, not only with his pen, but by direct person-to-person action, calling on the farmers one by one. It was easy to establish rapport with these, since he had shared their unhappy lot during the gras-hopper invasion. For a few weeks his activities were interrupted by the Black Hills excursion, but soon he was back from "beyond the Missouri," as he says, and deep in the "whirlpool of politics", where he labored with dedication and enthusiasm. How he worked the game is recorded in the sketch "Election Shenanigans," later in this book.

Wiśniowski's travels up and down and across our country have never been accurately traced, and it is probable they cannot be, down to the last detail. We do know, however, that he never stayed here very long at a time, as he never did anywhere, but journeyed back and forth to Europe and to his native country, ever the foot-loose adventurer. In Poland he wrote and lectured on his experiences and impressions and was always surprised at the reaction everywhere to what he had to say. Audiences were interested in our country, to be sure, but more interested in people they themselves had known who had migrated here. As Wiśniowski recalls,

> They ask you whether you knew N. N., who lives not far from Patagonia and works on an isolated farm as a shepherd. They are surprised if you don't know this N. N., and begin to doubt whether you were ever actually in America. Why, everybody there ought to know their beloved N. N., — such a fellow he was before he went out into the world. Why, — the whole of Polesie knew him![2]

Wiśniowski's last trip to the United States was in 1881. Three or four years later, with his wife, he returned for good to Poland, settling in Kolomyja as director of a factory and business man. Here he took active part in the political life of Eastern Galicia. Although he no longer wrote, he did, however, maintain cordial relations with the literary figures of his day, in particular with Jan Kasprowicz, at that time editor of *Kurier Lwowski*.

Wiśniowski was able, between his Far Western adventures and the final return home, to visit the West Indies, but not to realize his dream of journeying to the Far East. Nor did he live to an old age. His life, crowded to overflowing with adventures, ended in Lwów on the 23rd of April, 1892, when he was hardly more than fifty years old. Pneumonia carried him off after an illness of only two days. He left his American wife and an adopted daughter. Of the fate of these two, nothing is known, nor do we know what became of his unpublished writings and notes. They were probably lost, as was his name, also, for many years.

The translation which follows is but a beginning of what we hope may be serious studies of one of our most interesting Polish visitors. It has been made possible thanks to the publication in the 1950s of three volumes of stories and articles by Wiśniowski, selected and edited by Julian Tuwim and Bolesław Olszewicz. The three volumes are entitled, respectively, *Koronacja króla wysp Fidżi* (1953), *W kraju czarnych stóp* (1954), and *Dzieci królowej Oceanii* (1956). For our purposes we needed the first two of these volumes. The second, when we were unable to buy a copy in time, was kindly loaned us by Dr. R. Krystyna Dietrich, whose bibliographical researches embrace Wiśniowski, because of his translations of English verse into Polish. Material not found in the volumes mentioned was obtained from Warsaw through the courtesy of the Author's Agency, Michał Rusinek, Director.

Marion Moore Coleman

THE WONDROUS GOAL

A Fable of the New World

Poor little Jaś was an unhappy boy of eight. He was abused and mistreated. He could remember when it had been different, but that was long ago, when his own dear mother was alive.

Now all Jaś knew was unhappiness. His stepmother gave him only harsh words and tasks to do that kept him busy from early morning till late at night. Crusts of bread and thin broth were all he had to eat, with once in a long, long time a bowl of cabbage soup. Jaś was always hungry.

Jaś often thought how strange it was his own father had changed so. Once he had been kind and good, but now he never even noticed Jaś was alive. Finally Jaś decided there was nothing for him to do but run away. His father would never know, and his stepmother would be glad to have him out of the way. So every day Jaś saved a piece of the crust given him for dinner and hid it in a secret place in the barn.

When he had quite a little pile of the crusts, Jaś decided the moment had come to go. He put the dried crusts inside his shirt and waited for darkness. When night came and the moon had risen, Jaś stole out of the house. He walked and walked, not knowing where he was going, and not caring: it was anything to get away.

Finally Jaś began to be tired. He looked around for a place to rest, and a huge, barnlike building loomed up before him. At first he could see no door nor other opening, but then he discovered a door. It was closed, and Jaś had to pull hard to get it open. He peered inside.

As he peered, Jaś thought he heard a noise, and, full of fear, he darted inside the barn. In the corner stood an enormous barrel. Jaś gave a jump...and not a minute too soon, either, for the noise was now right behind him. Safe inside the barrel, he began to wonder where he was, and started feeling about in the darkness with his hand. There was an opening where a stave had been cut out, and through this Jaś could feel something soft. It came to him that the soft object was none other than the furry tail of a wolf. Jaś grasped the tail firmly and hung onto it.

And now the great adventure began. The wolf started running, the barrel and Jaś in tow. Faster and faster and farther and farther it ran, bumpity, bumpity, bump. Finally, with a thundering crash, the barrel landed against a gigantic tree. The staves flew in every direction, but Jaś, by a miracle, was not hit by one. Dusting himself off, the little boy got up and looked around. On the tree he saw a huge sign. He squinted his eyes and began reading. There was one word written on the sign, in great, huge letters.

The one word, the wonderful word was: AMERYKA.

SYGURD WISNIOWSKI

Tentative Chronology of His Life

1841	Born in Paniowce Zielone, Galicia, Austrian Poland.
Winter 1858	Leaves Stanislawow, where he was in school, for Turkey.
1859	Summoned home by his family, returns to the Stanislawow gimnasium. Completes studies here, then enters University of Lwow but does not complete studies here.
1860	Flees to Moldavia, thence to Sicily, hoping to serve under Garibaldi. Sicily already having been liberated, joins the Hungarian Legion and takes part in fighting around Naples.
February 1861	Serves in the Legion for a time, then goes to Genoa, to join the Polish group around General Ludwik Mieroslawski.
1862	Returns to Poland, but only briefly. Goes to London, and in June, 1862, sails for Australia. Arrives after a voyage of 95 days at Sydney.
End of 1862-1864	In various parts of New South Wales, always moving from place to place.
1864	Gets a job on the coal barge *Woodpecker*, plying from Newcastle, in eastern Australia, to Peru, where he visits the harbor of Callao. On return voyage lands in Auckland, New Zealand, and remains in New Zealand more than a year. Sees gold being mined.
1865	To escape being drafted for war with the Maoris, returns to Australia.
1865-68	In Victoria, New South Wales. Works on his own farm, near the village of Mudgee.
1868	Gets a job as cattle-tender on boat bound for the Fiji Islands.
1868-Spring, 1872	In Australia, mostly in Queensland in the gold mines. Involved in a mining venture in New Guinea. Saved from shipwreck.
Spring 1872	Leaves for England on the ship *Agnes Rose*.
Autumn 1872	In Poland briefly.
1873	Publishes in *Gazeta lwowska* sketches describing his ten years in Australia.
Spring 1873	In Switzerland. Visits Rapperswill.
Summer 1873	Boards the steamer *Minnesota* in Liverpool, bound for the United States. Visits Chicago.

1873	Excursion to Nebraska and Colorado.
Late 1873	Settles in New Ulm, Minnesota.
Summer 1874	Accompanies General Custer's 7th U. S. Cavalry to the Black Hills.
1875	Second excursion to the Black Hills. July 2 becomes editor of the *New Ulm Herald*.
Autumn 1876	In Warsaw.
March 1877	Leaves Warsaw for Galicia.
1878	On to England, then Paris. Meets Sienkiewicz at the Paris Exposition.
1879	In London. Then on to New York.
	Marries an American woman and engages in commercial activities.
	Visits Canada and the West Indies.
1881	On death of father, returns to Galicia, where he remains.
April 23, 1892	Dies in Lwow.

CONTENTS

	page
Introduction	i
The Wondrous Goal: A Fable of the New World	vi
Tentative Chronology of Wiśniowski's Life	vii
Sygurd Wiśniowski: A Portrait	xii

WIŚNIOWSKI'S AMERYKA

Writer as Missionary	2
The Polish Settler in the United States	5
A Better Life	6
The Letter from "Ameryka"	7
The Propaganda Arm of the Church	9
The Cincinnati Story	10
The Great God Business	12
Utopia beyond the Sea	13
Where Poles Have Settled Most	14
Echoes of the Custer-Black Hills Expedition	21
Reunion in Sioux City	22
Reporter Extraordinary	23
The Remarkable Sharp	25
A Mountain Achilles	26
Minnesota Sketches	29
How They Built a New Railroad	30
Petticoat Crusade	33
Plague of Grasshoppers	36
Election Shenanigans	40
Convention Trickery	43
Turning the Tide in Winona	48
Wisconsin: The New Poland	51

CONTENTS—Continued

LANGENOR

	page
Chapter One The Hermit of the Montana Wilderness	56
Chapter Two Comanche Bride	63
Chapter Three The Faithless Cheyenne	69
Chapter Four Escape from Emma	74
Chapter Five The Over-Eager Modiste	81
Chapter Six The Hero of Plum Creek	91
Chapter Seven Boarding House Elite	99
Chapter Eight Woman Trouble: White and Red	109
Chapter Nine Odyssey's End	115
Notes	123

Sygurd Wiśniowski

SYGURD WISNIOWSKI'S

AMERYKA

"Of America I don't need to write. The correspondence of Litwos [Sienkiewicz], Horain, and finally the stories and lectures of Wiśniowski and Benni, provide you with more precise news of this part of the world than I could..."

—Helena Modjeska, Letter to Maria Faleńska, San Francisco, April 27, 1877

2

WRITER AS MISSIONARY

Besides myself, you will find another Polish writer wandering about in the Wild West, one known to you all.[3] This immortal, more fortunate than myself, was not, as I, torn from the family nest in childhood, but as a mature man ventured forth on a pilgrimage, seeking to observe with his own eyes the most distant parts of the earth where our people are to be found.

This other wanderer came to these colonies of our fellow-countrymen with a full store of knowledge, as a professional writer, with a heart warm and noble, and with sufficient courage to enable him to triumph over every difficulty, whether of wind or weather, serpents, rocks, and evil men.

I possess neither the talent nor the pen of this man, who is able to depict people and places more graphically than an artist wielding the most skilful brush. And so, judging from what he has already written, though not knowing what he will produce in the future, I hereby advise readers who wish to hear the truth concerning our pioneers of the New World, to turn to the letters of this other traveler.[4]

Naturally no two writers dealing with half the earth will agree in their presentation of the people and conditions they encounter. In many ways my views, as those of a man of action and prose, will differ from those of the tourist-poet who, having wandered about the world, later writes in such a way as to remind you of an epic of Homer.

Still, I have no doubt that both men, the one of prose, the other of poetry, will agree in the main as to the character of the people living in the New World, and the fate of the colonists there. And so, let the letters of Sienkiewicz reveal what I can not, or do not know how to write on the subject.

You will ask, of course, why I have chosen as the principal theme of my sketches the subject I have mentioned, namely, the character of the people of the New World, and the fate of those who settle there. You will wonder why I have bored you with anecdotes from the life of the masses, and have remained silent on matters pertaining to that of the most elegant element of the elegant city.

Well, it is true that if I were seeking notice or acclaim, I would certainly choose a theme different from, say, the kitchen of a laboring man across the sea, or the woes of a local humorist. But I seek neither notice nor acclaim. Rather do I aim simply to perform to the full,—my duty.

Before the winds of life drove me to the wildest regions of the New World, and so forced me to live as brother with the rudest inhabitants of those regions, I was a subject of Austria. Then I freed myself legally of all duties to the government which had condescended to nurture me as a child. But I still retained, I can not deny it, a certain affection for those who, along with myself, dwelt under this government's aegis.

I recall that I was not unhappy in the wild regions to which life drove me. Nature enchanted me. I was fond of the people. I shared their fate, collecting material for future stories of oceans and volcanoes, of those who toil upon the sea, of two-legged moles cutting away at rocks, of the uncouth inhabitants of the sun-baked wilderness and of those dwelling in pine forests devoid of light.

My studies disturbed me only when they had to do with people of my own tongue. The majority of these one could hardly call "people." They were lost, frightful phantoms, without voice or color, without faith in either the world or God, not useful even to themselves, degrading themselves, and degraded. And as I listened to their moans, they kept appearing in ever greater numbers, ever more often. More than one, I found, was familiar with the very nest that had borne me!

From these creatures I came to know where and in what number the settlements of their fellow-countrymen were to be found. These I visited, all over the length and breadth of Europe, as I had the time and as strength and means permitted me. In my wanderings I experienced difficult ups-and-downs. Sometimes my journeying seemed the work of a missionary, who by the labor of his hands supports the work of his head, so that his spirit may be dedicated to the fulfillment of his purpose in life. I regret none of the hardships I have encountered, nor any of the hard work, since those experiences served to acquaint me with the aspect of settlement on the other side of the world which to me seemed the highest.

Free-willingly I paid the price exacted of every incautious emigrant from Europe to the New World: the moments of bitterness, the deceptions, the debasements. If I escaped the depths that lie in wait for most of our emigrants, it was because I had survived the novitiate of transplantation early in life, before the buoyancy and elasticity of youth had left me. At the time I did not feel the full severity of my situation and accepted whatever befell me, knowing that the experiences I endured would enable me later to soar, and to hold myself high above the abyss of denationalization.

Through it all, I held firm to the resolve that I would never break the most holy ties of family and nationality; that I would never become a living and walking "bad example;" that I would remember as much of my native speech as I could, so that some day I might be able to describe in that tongue the condition of people less fortunate than myself.

I regret that my journeys have so blunted my pen and warped my lips as to make me incapable of giving my words the impact of a slogan, the thundering force of a decree, the tenderness of adjurations to exhort, defend, beseech... To exhort that it is not necessary to leave the boundaries of one's own country and thus populate those of a new land; to communicate firmness to those whom fate has deposited among strangers; to adjure those mired in the sloughs of the New World to remember to their last ounce of strength that, immersing themselves in foreign elements, and rejuvenating already powerful races with their own poor, fettered nation, will bring no profit to those others, and only shame upon themselves.

This mission, the condition of our colonists from Galicia, Silesia, and other parts, in America, awakened in me.

THE POLISH SETTLER IN THE UNITED STATES

All sections of this portion of Wiśniowski's observations on American life were written while the author was living in New Ulm, Minnesota, and published in the Warsaw journal *Wędrowiec*, Nos. 38-41, 1877. They are to be found in the volume *Koronacja króla Wysp Fidżi*, Warsaw, 1953, pp. 328-57.

I. *A Better Life*

The fate of thousands of our colonists in the great cities of the eastern part of the United States has never differed very greatly from that of the poor European laboring man, nor does it today. You can count the number of people who have risen above the position of workers and servants in any city on the fingers of your hands. The saloon, the small shop, the pharmacy, the job of commercial clerk, which is the highest rank of the lowest official,—in these you have the whole aim of our people's ambition. When factories are working to the full and commerce is flourishing, they live better than at home. In bad times they suffer poverty and want more painful than anything they were accustomed to when young.

It was different with those who during the Civil War or in the years just following migrated westward. Conditions there in those years, and the participation of the people there in the war, opened the way to abundant profits for the foreigner. People of intelligence suffered, it is true, but those who worked at physical labor found profitable occupations and were able to use their hard-earned savings to buy land in places that were rapidly filling up or near cities growing overnight. As a result of the extensive railroad construction then going on, property out in the country purchased for a dollar and a half an acre went up to fifty or a hundred dollars. In Chicago, Milwaukee, and even smaller cities, lots bought for a hundred dollars with ten years to pay, before the final payment came due were worth several thousand. Land that when it was bought lay beyond the limits of town, in ten years was the site of the finest streets in the city. In this sudden rise in value of land bought for a little or nothing lies the explanation of the Kashubian, Silesian or Poznanian sections in various cities, or the stories you hear of how peasants unable to read or write today are worth many thousands of dollars.

These people combine an innate love of all the things their money can buy with boasts as to how they made their fortunes. Some of them, as they become rich, detach themselves completely from their fellow-countrymen and change their names, often in a manner that is ludicrous, but practical in the eyes of

Americans, whose tongues seem incapable of pronouncing our nasals and other sounds not found in the English language. To cite a couple of instances of the transformations that go on, there is the case of the crude little gander by the name of Łabuś who emerged in America as a butterfly with the French name La Buy. And for another, the owner of several stone buildings in a large city who didn't wish to be known as Szymonowicz and so adopted the euphonious Italian name Simonetti. It didn't do him any good, however, as I found when I had occasion to call at his tavern, which was the source of his fortune. My call had nothing to do with liquor, by the way. Anyway, I was greeted with harsh warnings in German that the proprietor did not accept people who preserve, as a kind of reliquary, the name and speech of their fathers. In return for this scorn of all things European, the Yankees still called him, in spite of his name, "a mean Dutchman," and looked down upon him, despising him for his awkward imitation of their customs.

II. *The Letter from "Ameryka"*

Besides giving themselves airs, people of this type,—and they number in the hundreds—love to write letters to their kinsmen and friends in Europe. I am familiar with this kind of correspondence, as I have written many such letters myself on behalf of illiterates. The letter has to begin usually with the words "Niech będzie pochwalony...[5]" etc., after which comes a catalog of what the writer possesses in land acreage, cattle, other livestock, and savings in the bank. News of the standing of His Magnificence mingles with word of any increase in the stable. Often there is enclosed with the letter a ten dollar bill or even a ticket purchased in New York for free passage from Hamburg to America, known in the strange nomenclature of these people, the "szyfkart."

This mania for writing letters, and I call it that advisedly, as well as the sending of tickets, is a more effective spur to emigration than all the persuasions of the agents of the Hamburg Steamship Company, who at a profit of ten or twenty percent a hundred on the price of tickets sold to unwary peasants, by word of mouth sow the idea of emigration. Letters arriving, written beyond question to persons known, or letters written by ne-er-do-wells who fled to America some years before in order to escape the hand of the law, not only exert a powerful effect on those to whom they are addressed, but fill the whole neighborhood with an entirely new train of thought. Pictures of an unknown Golconda[6] are enclosed in a crumpled piece of paper, smeared with hooks signed by the hand of a Bartek or a Wojtek.

The seed of desire to wander falls upon minds already freed by virtue of military service in Germany of the traditional timidity characteristic of a race that does not willingly leave the home nest. From German young people they have already heard of countries in which they can "better their fate." Conversations of this kind and the repetition of exaggerated descriptions of the good life to be enjoyed on the other hemisphere create themes for discussion and dreams, and become the inspiration for several years of intense saving, so that there may be money at hand for the journey. We think the home community is wedded to a settled life, but in this as in other aspects of our character, we fool ourselves.

From thousands of conversations with settlers sunk in the depths of American poverty, I have become convinced that the basis of their mad emigration was less the promises of foreign agents than the word sent home and the letters written in boastful speech, striking directly to the heart, telling of the success of persons they knew. These led to the illusory notion that in today's United States, filled to overflowing with the proletariat, there awaits the newcomer the "fortune" their predecessors found.

There isn't a peasant in Chicago who won't tell you the same story: how he came to the United States "to seek his fortune." But it is not easy to convince those yearning to cross the ocean of the betrayal awaiting them. To do so would require, besides general statements, irrefutable testimony in the form of letters from America written by persons known personally to those infected by the disease of wanting to get away. It would require, not poetically resounding pronouncements, or calls to a sense of duty to the homeland that does not exist, but steady work among individual would-be emigrants.

That warnings of danger to the emigrant's person restrain almost no one from leaving home, I have convinced myself, by investigations of my own at Castle Garden, where the emigrants land. In spite of pictures in the German press giving a distorted idea of conditions across the sea, emigrants landing in America are fully aware that as long as they live in populated neighborhoods, they have nothing to fear.

III. *The Propaganda Arm of the Church*

I have mentioned one spur to emigration, and shall mention another, also powerful, this one inspired not by foreign agents but by monsters of our own nation. I do not dare offer a cure for it but regard the open exposure of these evils as a duty, since what I shall say may turn the thinking of people who are familiar with conditions in Europe toward search for remedial measures to blot out various wrongs. Perhaps convince them that the time has come to stop declaiming about the machinations and wrong-doing of German agents and censure those who are more guilty than they and who do more harm.

One of the most powerful incentives to emigration of the German Catholics and of Catholic branches living next to them is the development of Catholicism in the United States. The spirit of propaganda and the desire to unite America for the Church has bound the Catholics there into a strong organization. This is so constituted that churches and parish buildings all belong directly to the bishops. And so the revenue from rich parishes serves often to strengthen countless settlements, either poor or in the process of forming.

The munificence of Catholics and, generally speaking, of all church members in America toward church aims, surpasses anything the European can conceive of. The state supports no one church, but the faithful are not sparing in their generosity toward the church and the clergy. It is no secret that in a given city there are to be found several hundred families with no allegiance to any church, or to any priest who would understand their confession, yet who stir up Catholics to give their brothers this spiritual help. Instances could be cited where Protestants have given both land and money for the building of Catholic churches. The existence of a church and school attracts settlers. School and church buildings create the nucleus of a new settlement. Population increase raises the value of land, and so in this way a contribution to a hated sect fills the pockets of the speculator.

I have called attention to this system of attracting settlers because it is an evil that can be overcome only through an understanding between the ecclesiastical authorities in Europe and the American bishops, perhaps in time to avoid mistakes in the choice of persons to whom permission is given to found a parish. As it is now, those given permission abuse the trust placed in them, luring people to emigrate, by means of letters and the printed word. A classic case of this was that of the famous priest Gurowski, who enticed peasants to Venezuela and then left them in Brussels to starve. He has so many imitators that they should really be stopped in their high-flying projects.

IV. *The Cincinnati Story*

The creation of a colony in Cincinnati, Ohio, affords an excellent example of the consequences of propaganda that depopulates the Catholic countries in the Old World in the illusion that the New World will render tribute.

A few years ago there came to Cincinnati a worthy priest. He was Father K...ski, a refugee from Italy at the time of the closing of the cloisters there. This clergyman was a very good wood carver, and so his relatives in Cincinnati had no difficulty in finding him work. There were, however, certain persons who looked upon the arrival of Father K and the liberality of the local Irish and German Catholics as an unexhaustible source of revenue, first through the collection of funds for the building of a church for a non-existent community, and second through managing the settlement that would inevitably collect around the church. These were people who weren't very literate, but endowed with that trickiness and irresponsibility which often help more in America than learning.

Father K, having distinguished himself from the general run of American priests by his garb, could not comprehend even the secondary plans of those who held his fate in their hands. Inspired by these persons with the idea of creating a new parish, he presented himself to Archbishop Purcell,[7] one of the most able and important American prelates. He asked him for the privilege of collecting money for the purpose. The privilege was granted and his endeavors among American Catholics brought him enough for a deposit on a Lutheran church that was for sale.

The rest of the money needed for the purchase of the church was quickly collected in the usual manner of that community, by balls, lotteries, and social events in which beer flowed copiously and the maidens of the community sold kisses to the young men making the highest bid. This transformation of the house of God into a tavern is one of the unpleasant sides of colonization in the western hemisphere.

In order, however, that wealthy persons might frequent the various fund-raising events, it was necessary to have a parish to display. And so letters were written to Europe, embroidered with gold and silver fairy tales. The dust of the streets in Cincinnati contained banknotes, and factories whistled with invitations to those across the sea. And those beyond the ocean came. Their homespun coats, their customs, submissiveness, and poverty surprised and amused the reporters and readers of American papers. Their kinsmen who had been living in Cincinnati for a long time did not have the means to help these newcomers, and so they were to be found sleeping under the sky, in city squares, parks, or under bridges. Eventually the peasants found the lowest type of work. There is in Cincinnati a dye factory, which employs this type of laborer exclusively, as it pays them half what it has to give other laborers and tyrannizes over them besides. While engaged in this kind of work, the family, with grown sons and daughter, crowds into a single tiny hut. They make their own furniture, packing cases and kegs taking the place of tables and chairs. Their principal articles of food are ribs, bought for almost nothing in the gigantic slaughter houses of the city, where every winter they slaughter millions of pigs for the market. Bones that have been thrown away and the meat that clings to these the people collect and salt down, to tide them over the summer. They regard this as healthful and tasty food.

I often talked with these people and asked them what they hoped for in coming to America. They sad that they had been told in letters that in Cincinnati every peasant receives at the least two dollars a day. And now they were paid only one dollar, and even then there was no steady work. Also, they had read in the printed works and newspapers which were sent them that America was a "free country," which they translated to mean that they did not even have to bow to a priest if they did not wish to. With this their conception of the privileges of the chosen sons of America ended. Besides, they could not enjoy other privileges since, fearing military service in case of war, they did not take out citizenship papers.

The dwellings of these immigrants reminded me of descriptions I had read of the poorest dens of London, Berlin and Vienna. A family consisting of father, mother, and grown children of both sexes, plus two unmarried boarders taken in to help pay the rent, would be found crowded into a tiny hut. And yet it must be confessed that, while living under such unsavory conditions, the sober portion of this population set something aside every week, even if only a dollar, for the church and for its own future. The amount collected went for the most part to the archbishop, for church purposes. Since the salary of the priest as well as other religious expenses are covered in America by money collected from pew rentals, almost every Polish family in Cincinnati paid five dollars a quarter for a pew with five seats. In more wealthy communities the rental was higher.

V. *The Great God Business*

Even the evil of ill-treating the immigrants under the pretext of increasing the Catholic element in America pales in the face of another practice, or rather knavery. Some persons, after collecting as much money in the New World as they can, abandon even the first principles of honesty and uprightness.

Business becomes the watchword of these people, the dollar their deity. They are a hundred times worse than the Yankees, who are held back by fear of their relatives and neighbors. They conspire by means of letters, pronouncements either printed or made personally with a European people, wherever they are richest, to lure the peasant to unpopulated and often barren parts of the country, where they sell them American acres. They transport him to Texas, to replace the Negroes there. Some weeks ago I received a letter from one of these operators. He boasted that he had six hundred thousand acres for settlement, and asked me whether I couldn't supply him with Polish peasants for the purpose. Undoubtedly he expected to set them to picking cotton, while he stood over them with a revolver in his hand. He probably thought their labor would be cheaper than that of the Negroes. Worst of all in this, the fellow bore the name of a brother of good standing, who fought stubbornly against peasant emigration. He kept that name until he took on one with a German-American sound. He promised to call on me in the spring in the hope of making some kind of deal. I trust he will come, so that I can tan his hide.

VI. *Utopia Beyond the Sea*

A disaster of another kind I call the emigration of the Utopians, who come seeking in the New World a place in which to create a new Icaria.[8] Usually they arrive with a plan of some rural colony and dreams of an idyllic life, which it is harder to find in America than hunting adventures, or brawls or professions. The machine-oriented nature of the American economy, the high cost of service and, as a result of the latter, the necessity of doing the hardest kind of work with one's own hands, soon spoil the bucolic idyll for them. Before My Lady has used up her first pair of arm-length gloves, brought from Europe to use in milking the cows, they have fled to the city. Here they try out a life of idleness, reaping the scorn people there have for the lazy and idle. Generally they return to the old world with great regret for America, that is, if they have enough to get back. If they don't have this, then the fate of the intelligent proletarian awaits them, of which I have spoken earlier.

The different and varied desires of the immigrants, whether peasants or artisans, and the intelligentsia as well, bring profit to the speculators, generally to those who know how to discuss their dreams in the immigrants' own language. Germans lure Germans across the sea, Italian agents travel about Italy, and in almost every American city of any size are to be found Polish offices distributing Polish pamphlets about Europe in which the climate and other inducements in the colonies to be settled are presented in glowing terms. They write most often of the climate, and least often about what the emigrant is to fill his stomach with. They do not forget to enumerate the privileges of citizenship, but leave out entirely other privileges such as the freedom to die of hunger if the emigrant is not willing to lower himself to begging.

Every newspaper publishes ads of the emigration offices and colonization companies, offering in disgusting language their "szyfkarty" for transportation "across the sea," or for some miraculous Radom [a Polish town in Illinois], or endless expanse of land in Iowa on which thousands of families of one nationality may buy land for almost nothing. These newspaper ads I can not sufficiently condemn. Publishers justify themselves for accepting them on the ground that they need the business, that universal excuse of people without conscience. They say that in America when it's a question of business, or personal interest, anything goes. There can be no doubt that a few samples of such publications, which in fact are shipped to Europe in quantities, do more harm than a German agent. They are serpents crawling among naive people under a deceptive name.

VII. *Where Poles Have Settled Most*

Having noted so many times the misery of the settlers, I will run over the most important settlements, scattered over the enormous expanse of America. I have often been asked in which parts and in what regions of the United States are to be found the colonies of which strange reports are often carried to the old country. And I reply with a question of my own: in which state and city are there not people to be found of whom reports are sent?

And so in New York City there are about ten thousand artisans and peasants of Polish origin and but a couple of dozen more wealthy Poles. In Philadelphia there are several hundred families, in Hartford in the state of Connecticut, in Newark, New Jersey, as well as in the cities around New York, all these totaling up to several hundred families in all. A considerable number of these people work in shoe factories, many also are occupied in horticulture.

In New York as in Chicago, though on a smaller scale, are organizations, not, however, with many members. They have their reading rooms, and also put on amateur theatrical performances, which, thanks to the endeavors of certain individuals, you could hear in local towns of the provinces. Even in Philadelphia they make a travesty of little Polish comedies. Americans attend these performances out of curiosity, Polish Jews in order to hear a familiar sound. A distinguished Philadelphia rabbi visited a first performance. I was told that honest and upright Jews filled the hall and their faces were lined with tears, expressive of feelings they could not utter, despite the absolute parody they were watching on the stage!

In this city of Philadelphia live three Remaks,[9] Jews from Poznań, who were brought to America as infants. All three are distinguished attorneys. They don't understand a word of Polish. One of them is high up in the Republican party and president of the famous Fairmount Park. At our gatherings they speak English. And to show you that there is nothing in America without its comic side, one of the brothers fulminates for the Democrats, another for the Republicans.

In New York, Newark, as well as in Chicago and other cities, our people amuse themselves in the militia. Tavern keeper N. N. hands out several kegs of beer on the day a battalion is organized and officers are chosen. They fill out the staff ranks by elections. The government provides outdated muskets. There are few private soldiers and not many are needed, as this army is not for war.

In some communities there are demagogues who deliver votes wholesale to American candidates. The people out in the country, making up their own minds, incline on the whole to the Democratic camp, mainly because of the influence of the Irish, with whom they are linked by religious ties. The link has become stronger since President Grant inaugurated his American Kulturkampf.[10] Dreaming of a third term as president, which by tradition is forbidden, he decided to set Catholics at odds against Protestants. And so his clique made the school question, which by its very nature belongs to the communities and states, the slogan of party extremists. The maneuver did not turn out to be a complete success, but it lost the Republicans many Catholic supporters.

Republican Catholics formerly followed the lead of Archbishop Purcell of Cincinnati. This prelate supported Lincoln and the enfranchisement of the Negroes, but from the time of the school quarrels he left the Republicans.

Polish artisans, as protectionists, incline in part to the Republicans. The intelligentsia is divided, but the majority, like the same group among Germans and Americans, are to be found in the Republican camp.

The one and only useful Polish school in the eastern states, and generally speaking in all America, is in Buffalo, at the point where the Niagara River flows into Lake Erie. Thanks to the dedication of the distinguished pastor there,[11] although his parish numbers but around seven hundred families, more than four hundred children attend this school.

As to this question of schools, I will repeat what Peter Kiołbassa,[12] delegate from Chicago to the Illinois legislature, wrote me. In his letter he confirms my own conviction, arrived at on the basis of my own research, that our people who have settled in America neglect the education of their children worse than any other racial groups, acting in this as if distaste for learning were an inborn characteristic. It would tear your heart to hear the words of scorn heaped by him on the Polish communities for their treatment of the school. Of course it must be added here that there are almost no Polish schoolmasters in America capable of teaching the Polish-American child. Such a teacher has in truth to be a genius, to read and write Polish, German and English, to be an organist, to know how to get along with the pastor, to unite the majority of the parishioners and to please the old grandmothers. Even Chicago has had no decent school since they got rid of the teacher who was at the same time editor of the first good-size Polish-American newspaper that didn't go bankrupt.[13] Only the school I have mentioned in Buffalo can be called a useful establishment. In other places there are Sisters teaching who neither understand English nor are able to maintain discipline. The lack of teachers, or rather the unwillingness to look for any, ruins the minds of our Polish-American children. Our people can not send their children to schools of mixed nationality and do not wish to follow the example of the Irish and establish expensive schools of their own faith. And so their children grow up to be ignoramuses, though the American environment supplies them a little polish and business knack.

In Pittsburgh, that Sheffield of America, there is a good-size community and church. In Shamokin, also in Pennsylvania, as well as in the surrounding country, peasants from East Prussia perform the very hardest labor in the coal mines. This group of people was so wise as to return to Prussia during a period of unemployment in the mines, and when good times returned to America to cross the sea again. I met this whole group on my last journey from New York to Hamburg and learned from them that they regarded going back and forth across the ocean as all in the day's work. In Lykens, also in Pennsylvania, there was quite a Polish colony. Not long ago there was a bad fire there that destroyed the whole settlement.

In the vicinity of Shamokin (Pennsylvania) there are two Latvian colonies, with priests and churches. These are not the only parishes of this kind in the United States. In Detroit, the commercial capital of the state of Michigan, on the St. Clair River, several thousand Poles are to be found. As everywhere, so here, Kashubians, Poznanians and Silesians, etc., have a tendency to keep apart, coming together only in the church. In Detroit there was a Polish newspaper which later was moved to Chicago,[14] and there is a bookstore whose catalogue is very interesting.

Going farther west by way of St. Louis, in the state of Missouri we find many rich Polish farmers. In Union City there is a monastery of the Resurrectionists. Here there was published for several years a journal called *The Pilgrim*.[15] Later this was changed into a considerable paper, and moved to Detroit. At present it appears in Chicago.

Relatively speaking, the greatest number of Poles is to be found in the beautiful state of Illinois. Here, [in the south-central part of the state] is to be found a new Radom. In South Bend, in the state of Indiana but very close to Chicago, several hundred pairs of Polish hands are engaged in manufacturing machines that will find their way eventually as far as Warsaw. In Chicago itself there are more than 20,000 Poles. They have three churches, two schools, nine clerical brotherhoods, a club known as Gmina and a Catholic literary association, to say nothing of two weekly papers and one monthly.

In Chicago I met very distinguished Polish priests[16] as well as several of somewhat lesser stature. The thirteenth, fourteenth and seventeenth districts of this commercial capital of the state are occupied chiefly by Silesians and Poznanians, who, as is well known, have elected their own kinsman, Mr. Kiołbassa, to the state legislature of Illinois.

As to the Chicago press, I do not wish to expatiate on this at length. I have already called attention to its carelessness in filling its pages with the proclamations of emigration agents and colonization companies. It would be hard to expect anything better from them, since their publishers look upon journalism as a business, nothing more. They think it requires no knowledge beyond the ability to set type. I have to confess that in this respect they share the conviction of most American editors of small publications, who create and set their articles at the compositor's desk.

The political influence of the Polish-American press amounts to nothing, since the majority of readers are well aware that the papers change their opinions according to the views of the publisher, who has his eye fixed on the party that will pay to get its pronouncements in print. I recall how one of these publications, with a conservative title, publicized the opinions of the

German Socialist paper, which had a circulation in America of hundreds of thousands of copies, in the desire to accommodate itself to the mass of Polish workers.

Once I asked the publisher of another paper, by conviction a Republican, why he supported the election of a poor German demagogue by the name of Hesing, editor of the anti-Polish *Illinois Staatszeitung*.

"He gave me an ad, my dear fellow," the editor replied, "and it's business first and foremost."

It wasn't long afterward that Hesing was hauled into court for having participated in a plot that involved even the secretary of President Grant.

The various Polish newspapers quarrel among themselves... of course, where are there newspapers that don't do this? One editor calls another a "bubas" or a "laufer." "Bubas" comes from the German *Bube*, rogue, and "Laufer," also German, literally "a runner," refers to a fellow who frequents taverns, never orders a drink (that has to be paid for), but eats all the goodies offered free to permanent American drinkers: a "freeloader," in other words. These taunts suit the Polish speech of the readers. The poor American Polish peasant tells you when he is going out into the country that he "jedzie na *kuntry*." If you ask him where he works, he will tell you "przy *stymowej* pile" (at the *steam* saw-mill). Bad meat he calls, "same knochy," —nothing but bones, from the German *Knochy*, bones.

Here is a sample of the printed style:

> Jan N. N., age 40, stood at the gate. A large wagon approached and could not get through the gate. The cart broke Jan N. N.'s skull, leaving a wife and four children, the youngest only six month's old.

The paper didn't make it clear whether it was the cart that left the children or Jan N. N.

Chicago serves more often than any other center as the meeting place of delegates gathering annually from the various communities for the so-called conventions of the different organizations. They come together in order to discuss means of founding a seminary for teachers and priests, and to collect money for these projects. So far nothing has come out of their debates, though there have been meetings of the delegates several times in Detroit, Milwaukee, and Chicago. Representatives of the brotherhoods, associations and parishes take part in these meetings. At these meetings you will find mostly priests. Judging from the number of representatives, I should say that the number of communities feeling the need of such common action does not exceed forty. Others do not concern themselves sufficiently to have conventions. Their members attend the German or Irish churches or none at all.

As to settlements besides those I have mentioned, there are others: in feverish Indiana, in murderous South Carolina, in rascally Arkansas, in productive Iowa and Kansas, everywhere I met groups of people intermarrying with Germans, living often in poverty, sometimes fairly prosperous, and lost in the German element.

Besides the state of Illinois, the principal fields of settlement of Prussian and Galician Poles have been Texas in the south and Wisconsin in the north. Texas I have never visited, but I know that there you will find the oldest of our settlements, such as Częstochowa and Panna Maria,[17] founded as Polish colonies twenty years ago.

I shall speak at greater length of Wisconsin elsewhere.

ECHOES OF THE CUSTER-
BLACK HILLS
EXPEDITION

I. *Reunion in Sioux City*

It was in the spring, and I was in Sioux City. Before I had circulated about more than five minutes, I knew that the most interesting experience was to be had, not in town, but on the outskirts, and on the other side of the river, in the camp of the adventurers who, taking a neutral stand, in defiance of the government in Washington, were massing in order to journey five hundred miles and perambulate along Custer's flank. And so I found a raft and made for the other side, amid logs and floating ice cakes.

Cold and tired, I leapt out of my little boat, which resembled a New Zealand canoe, and like a Maori myself hopped from one log to another, until finally I reached the bank. There I climbed a hill and was struck right in the eye by the prairie wind, on the very top of the prairie as I was. Avoiding the army encampment, assembled there to keep an eye on the miners, I proceeded to a group of twenty-five carts, the prairie schooner type, placed so as to form a quadrangle. In these wagons I knew was to be found the largest band of the Black Hills fanatics.

Five minutes after I had arrived at the camp and presented myself as a newspaper reporter and ex-gold-miner, I had, with the aid of a bottle of whiskey and a gift for making friends with rapscallions, won the confidence of several of the outstanding members of the expedition. When, moreover, I told them that I had been with Custer in the Black Hills, and that I had with my own hands panned gold there, also that I was sure that in time there was money to be made there, I was accorded a seat of honor by the fire and given something to eat. I was surrounded on all sides, and what I told them was listened to with the intensity you find in the west....

I had hardly finished my account of the gold obtained by the Custer party and a description of that gold, when a bald head detached itself from the mass of heads and bent forward. A face that I had seen before grinned at me, revealing a mouthful of blackened and uneven teeth. The owner of these, whom I knew by sight from my previous year's journey, had probably been a muleteer or military teamster at that time, and so I had had no intimate contact with him. But his reputation had reached my ears, since the owner of that bald head and thin, shaven face and black teeth was the greatest liar not only in Custer's army but in all the country between the Missouri and the Black Hills. In order to win the distinction of Greatest of All Liars, in this country of mighty yarn-spinners, one had to have a real calling for the art, and not just a modest imagination.

Old Pete, as he was known, or Pete the Liar, as hundred-mouthed Rumor dubbed him, grasped my big, rough hand with one still rougher and bigger and also blacker. He took a seat beside me, as if he too deserved a place of honor, and started making up to me, as if a reporter and wagon-driver belonged to one and the same category. Loosening the reins of his lively imagination, he began telling me tall tales of the Black Hills, looking me straight in the eye as he did so. He described the hunting forays there, the nuggets of gold as big as a child's head that were found, and other phenomena you could never imagine. Actually his recital was directed not just to me but to the entire crowd, but whenever it seemed to him that his listeners were inclined to doubt his word, he would turn to me for confirmation and ask, "That's so, isn't it?"

I had never in my life been in just such a situation. Pete had a revolver, I only a stick. Pete was known for his prowess in a brawl, for me life had started pleasantly. Pete liked to lie, I am not fond of suporting people in their lies. Pete sat there right next to me, however, and what could I do but nod assent.

[*Kłosy*, 550, p. 32]

II. *Reporter Extraordinary*

Pressing my hand, Pete began to boast.

"I tell you," he said, "I got half a pound of gold out of every pan of earth out there in Custer Park. I can prove it, for when it was weighed, all the reporters were standing there beside me. This fellow here was probably one of them and he'll certainly remember that the last nugget weighed half a pound, give or take a little sand. I have to admit that we weren't always exact, and when it weighed half a pound or a quarter of a pound over, we'd sprinkle a little sand for balance. That's right, isn't it, sir?"

"Well now, I don't remember exactly how it was, as I was busy with other things just at that time," I begged off.

"There's a reporter for you," Pete came back, incredulous, "a fine reporter, that! Why, when I was a reporter for the *New York Herald*, when a fly buzzed in the midst of one of Daniel Webster's six-hour-long orations, down there in Congress, I took that buzz right down in shorthand, sir: BZZ. Old Bennett [James Gordon Bennett, the *Herald's* owner] told me he never had so exact a reporter as Old Pete. Of course he paid me well for that! How he did pay!"

"Then why did you leave the *Herald*?" one of the miners asked.

"Well, what happened was, they sent me to New Orleans to report on the yellow fever that was carrying off a thousand people a day," Pete replied. "People were dying like flies, and every burial had to be noted. I couldn't keep up, though I wrote all night long. So I quit. Finally I got the fever myself, and since that time I haven't had a quarter of my old strength. Before that I could lift a horse right up off the ground. I had the fever a long time, and didn't get rid of it until it got scared out of me. That cured me. It happened when I was riding across a long bridge, going from the levee to one of the plantations near New Orleans. I was riding in a rough cart and it was dark. You could hardly see. I had got right up to the bridge, and here the whole floor was gone, carried away by the flood..."

The rest of Pete's story told how he managed to cross that bridge, by making his horses jump from one bare support to another. The experience was so harrowing that it scared the fever right out of him.

[*Kłosy*, 550]

III. *The Remarkable Sharp*

There was a dog in camp that strongly appealed to me. It was a full-blooded rat terrier, an English breed, better than a half dozen cats, still young, and so capable of being trained, the very dog I had been seeking for a long time.

"Whose is he, that dog?" I inquired.

"Old Pete's."

"Would he sell him?"

"I doubt it," my guide around the camp shook his head. "The old liar loves dogs and has half a dozen of them, but this one, Captain Jack he calls him, is his favorite."

I couldn't get over wanting the dog. And so, against all good judgment, I went to the old liar and very diplomatically communicated to him the question as to whether he might not be willing to sell this namesake of the King of the Modocs.[18]

"Never!" Peter exploded. "Sell him? Never! Why, Captain Jack is the last descendant of a famous race, the only one bred in America. His father, Old Sharp, why he could kill a hundred and twenty rats a minute. He did it once in New York, in the hall that everyone knows who's interested in that sport. And he won a big bet for me!"

"Aw, go on, you're exaggerating," someone objected.

"Not exaggerating at all," Old Pete came back, looking his challenger straight in the eye. "And if you don't believe it, just listen. I put him in a hole in the room where the test was made, and then I threw a whole cask full of rats into it. Sharp took his stand at the bung hole of the cask. Every time a rat stuck his head out to get a breath of air, Sharp would strangle him. The rats finally began to pour out too fast, so that Sharp had one in his jaws and two in each paw at the same time. Well, sirs, with this he stuck his tail into the bunghole and shut the rats right up in the cask. After he had disposed of those that had got outside, he pulled out his tail and got rid of the rest. In that way he finished them all off in a minute. But poor Sharp! He had worked so hard at killing those rats that the next day he died of apoplexy. How could I ever sell the descendant of a creature whose manly prowess won me a thousand dollars?"

But I was determined, and with the help of many draughts of whiskey won Pete's friendship so that in the end he gave in and sold me the last scion of the redoubtable Sharp for five dollars.

[*Klosy*, 551]

IV. *A Mountain Achilles*

In Deadwood City, in the Black Hills, the most impressive person was Wild Jack. He was a very mountain Achilles. I ran into him first in Cincinnati, where his enormous stature and picturesque garb made him an object of wonder. A real superman, Jack was handsome, in a classical way. Tall, blond, with long, wavy hair and heavy beard, he was not the loud-mouthed, roistering mountain man of fiction, but modest and restrained, though always sure of himself. Under his embroidered jacket you could see the glistening handles of two revolvers, and his blue eyes glistened too, with courage and honesty.

In Deadwood, when not leading parties through the hills, Jack occupied himself organizing a Committee of Safety. Actually Jack was himself the Committee of Safety, the one called upon to arbitrate every dispute, and it was in line of duty that he met his death.

Another leading figure in Deadwood, and a real frontier character, was Major Merryweather, editor of the *Black Hills Avalanche*. Where Merryweather got his military title no one knew, perhaps from membership in the Minnesota militia. He came to Deadwood from Custer City, carrying on a mule and his own back full equipment for a printing establishment. Included in the equipment were, of course, revolvers and knives for defense.

With a couple of helpers and a local boy, Editor Merryweather set himself up in a shaky old building, open to rain and snow, but with one good feature: a strong outside door which could be barred securely from within, and a peephole through which the boy could see an approaching intruder. Merryweather did not hesitate to let himself go editorially against wrongdoers, even if they were his neighbors, and such precautions were necessary.

Merryweather might have been short on logic and grammar, but he could write a human interest story that would wring your heart, and he was a master of the crude humor of the west. His *Avalanche* stood ready to publish anything that was news, from ads for a newly arrived cargo of flour, to tears over the dead, or serious opinions on government and the courts. For his feature articles and editorials he had a whole library of clippings to draw on, and when, for example, a prominent citizen died, the piece carried by the *Avalanche* was but a remake of one of Daniel Webster's great eulogies.

To everyone's regret, Merryweather was killed in a duel with a rival editor, a Colonel (?) Lansborough who arrived in the Black Hills from Bismarck in Dakota Territory with two wagonloads of printing equipment, prepared to give Deadwood a "new style" newspaper. After a period of bitter competition, there was a duel, a Hamilton-Burr affair, in which, according to old-timers in Deadwood, Lansborough was actually guilty of murder.

The feeling against Lansborough was so intense that the Committee of Public Safety felt it necessary to act. Only Wild Jack was bold enough to carry out the Committee's decree that he should be jailed. There was a prison of sorts in Deadwood, and here Jack locked Lansborough in. His friends tried at once to break through and rescue the prisoner, but failed, and in their frustration went after Jack.

The avenging band found Jack quietly sitting in one of Deadwood's many gambling houses, and there, before he could defend himself, they shot him in the head. Lansborough was let go free.

Mourning for the slain Jack was sincere and profound. As his coffin was lowered into the frozen ground, friends threw in his two silver-handled revolvers. There was not a dry eye in the crowd.

"We all loved him," said the spokesman for the townspeople, "he was a good man. He never turned away from his door a man in need. He was swift as lightning if attacked, but mild as the spring rain in dealing with friends. Peace be to his soul. The West will not soon see his equal."

[*W kraju czarnych stóp*, abstract of pp. **100-106**]

MINNESOTA SKETCHES

The first five sketches that follow are to be found in the volume *Koronacja króla Fidżi*, pp. 245-48; 267-72; 282-85. Eventually all were published in *Kłosy* during the years 1874-75. The sixth sketch is to be found in *Kłosy*, No. 597, p. 359.

MINNESOTA SKETCHES

I. *How They Built A New Railroad*

In the state of Minnesota, of which I am a citizen, and where they already have a more extensive network of railroad lines in this year of our Lord 1874 than are to be found in any part of Austria, there is a province with the typical rolling and uneven surface of the western prairie, and barren of firewood. The capital of this part of the state, New Ulm,[19] a city of two thousand people, half of them Germans, lies in the midst of a wooded spot of several hundred morgs.[20] A little farther on in the province, beside a small stream winding in and out of a grove, several hundred farming families have settled. Farther to the west you find in summer nothing but grasshoppers and prairie fires, and in winter piles of snow driven straight from the North Pole by winds as fierce as tropical hurricanes and so bitter cold that in half an hour they can kill cattle, and even the most warmly clad human being. At this time of year all you see is a vast white waste. In spring a sea of green grass, with the bones of buffaloes whitening here and there, in places great numbers of these, though whether they died because of the much greater severity of the climate in those particular areas, or from the activities of hunters, I can not say.

Two hundred miles farther west, on prairie land still inhospitable to man, are to be found, according to trappers who have been hunting there, deposits of coal so rich that you can see the brownish veins above the surface of the low hills and on the steep slopes of canyons. Whether these mines exist or not, or reside only in the lively imagination of the pioneers, who are always looking for coal or gold and copper, I can again not say for sure. In our neighborhood little faith is put in such stories.

By a group of stockholders in Chicago, the financial capital of our part of the world and the native habitat of the most daring business men in the country, full credence was placed in these riches of coal said to be found out there on the prairie, and as yet unseen by human eye. Not moving one step from the exchange, and not spending a cent on engineers or prospectors to see whether there was really any coal or not, these brokers formed a company to get the concession for building a railroad from New Ulm to the place where the mines were alleged to be. They also dreamed of extending the line three hundred miles beyond, to the banks of the Missouri, provided their stockholders would supply the funds in the hope of future riches.

The men engaged in the project plead their case this way:

> Even if we don't find any mines, on both sides of the line is a prairie just waiting to be put under cultivation, and the only reason it has not been taken up before this is its lack of wood. The railroad will be able to carry the building material that will be needed from the east, and sell it to the farmers on both sides of the line. The freight charges received from this, plus what we take in from the wheat that will be transported from the west, will not pay dividends to the investors, but will give us directors at least a good return. The considerable strip of land on both sides of the right of way, which the government will give us, will at first be of little value, but in time will increase in value so that the heirs of the investors will get rich by selling it. And so "the wolf will be satisfied and the sheep remain whole."[21]

...The promoters' engineer, full of energy and truly a man of genius, never bothered his head with surveying the road, but, in full confidence that if he went due west he would eventually reach the banks of the Missouri, proceeded to set ploughs and scrapers to work. Two wide, deep trenches, running parallel to each other twelve feet apart, marked out the course. The earth turned up from these trenches was heaped in the middle to provide a base for the future rails and ties. Right across the low hills of the prairie ditches were made, the higher mounds were passed in very bold arcs. Baskets of earth and bundles of willow twigs were thrown into the marshy places. Here and there viaducts were built over them, on palings sunk but a couple of feet into the marsh.

Except for the bridge near New Ulm, which crossed a considerable river, and so had to be built of well-constructed piers, the whole job went very quickly, until the panic of last autumn[22] halted it. Before a hundred miles of the road had been completed, the money gave out, and, what was worse, the stockholders who had been so easily duped, came to their senses. And so the railroad ended up, as they say, in the air, half way to the promised land of coal, on a prairie as wild and silent as the Sahara.

Several hundred pioneers, among them your correspondent, more out of love for the life of a hermit than for visions of profit, had built their little homes and shelters on the two sides of the eastern portion of this railroad line.[23] We sowed wheat, most of which was devoured by prairie dogs, grasshoppers, and the various birds of the prairie, no less numerous and destructive than the grasshoppers. What was left after they had eaten their fill, we sent to New Ulm by the railroad, which we ourselves almost never used. With the exception of rare and unforeseen accidents, we always went to the city ourselves on horseback, following a road that paralleled the rails, racing the trains from time to time, and even beating them.

An unforeseen incident forced me, in the last days of February, to leave my horses in the care of neighbors and journey some two hundred miles beyond New Ulm. A friend, working in the pine forests to the north, was accidentally injured, and wrote me, asking me to come and take care of his business affairs, which, as he said, his wife was incapable of doing. It was too late in the season to make so long a journey on horseback or by sleigh, and so, willy-nilly, I had to go by way of our railroad.

Except for the conductor and engineer, I had no one to share my misery. Shaken to pieces on that rough and uneven road, I felt like someone tossed about in a cart without springs. I can not describe my sufferings and fears: would the viaduct fall into the marsh or the locomotive leap from the rails. Finally, alive and whole, I reached a river over which a bridge had been built. And so we got out of the train and the two of us, the conductor and I, crossed the ice on foot.

The piers of the bridge were supposed to have been constructed of brick. The businessmen in Chicago, not wishing to lose time and money in building under the water, waited until the coldest part of winter when three feet of ice covered the river, and built the piers on the ice.

Four posts, nineteen to twenty feet high, stood on the surface of the ice. As soon as the posts reached the required height, the workmen cut the ice all around and lowered the posts into the water. A few feet will show above the quagmire, and on these they lay the part of the piers that are supposed to support the wooden bridge. Since the piers have no foundations, every year they must of course sink into the mire, into the bottom of the river, and every year they have to be raised up.

Such a system not even Brassey[24] or the Lwów-Czernowitz Company ever thought of! That idea was strictly American, teaching even us, who are citizens of the most ingenious nation in the world, a lesson in recklessness.

The conductor told me, in the course of the journey, that the engineer had no idea where the rails were to be laid more than three or four miles ahead of the workmen. Fortunately, on this flat prairie, it was not easy to take the wrong route. But who knows whether, when the road is finished, if it ever is, it will reach the desired goal of the Missouri, or some other!

II. *Petticoat Crusade*

For several months the women of Ohio and Indiana had carried on a new campaign to force the saloon-keepers to close their shops. Directed by several apostles of prohibition, crowds assembled, marched about the streets, visited saloons, and delivered sermons to the saloon-keepers. They even bought up, wholesale, the various beverages on sale in the saloons, and poured them into the sewers.

The movement took root and spread, even to distant Minnesota, where every town has its brewery and every second building in every town is a saloon. In New Ulm we had fifty-three saloons to serve our two thousand inhabitants.

I had been in Duluth, and now was returning to Minneapolis, a city of thirteen thousand inhabitants, rivalling St. Paul in commercial supremacy, and as richly supplied with tramways and German beer-gardens as the capital.

The crusade began seriously in Minneapolis among the American part of the population. A minister of the Methodist Church arrived in Minnesota from the east and started a movement among the women, both rich and poor, to drive out the saloons. A crowd of people gathered around these women, curious to know what they were up to, and some joined with them. The English press praised their work, the German condemned it with one voice, declaring that no crusade and no proclamation would ever change drunkards into sober citizens, and that if they forbade the taverns to sell liquor, opium would take its place, the way it had already done in states that had adopted statutes against drinking.

The modest Polish inn in which I was stopping belonged to the host, who very unwillingly was obliged to sell vodka and beer. He himself told me that he would gladly give up the profit derived from this traffic, if the neighboring hotels did not dispense strong liquors.

"Children and wives learn to drink beer," he told me, "and can become drunkards. And so I wish I could drive out of my house the everlasting temptation to weak souls. But if I did, I would lose my guests, and the only result would be that my competitors would profit."

A half hour after our conversation the postman brought a card announcing that today the crusading women would visit my host and try to persuade him, by plea and prayer, to close his saloon. The poor fellow waited with pounding heart for the promised visit, though his wife, a Polish woman, tried to comfort him, and urged him to slam the door in the face of the fanatical women.

"I wouldn't let those hydras into the saloon!" she cried.

She had hardly uttered the words when thirty women, different types, but in general of good appearance, and even elegantly dressed, appeared on the street and without hesitation entered the saloon, which up to then had been empty. One of them began a long oration, full of quotations from the Bible. All this was in bad German, as the women knew my countryman did not speak English. Praising him to the sky if he would hand over the key to the cellar, and cursing him to the nether regions if he refused, the women tried to get him to promise not to sell liquor in the future. Thanks to the firmness of his wife, he did not sign, despite the fact that the women offered him a good price for the whole stock of liquor that he had on hand.

The women knelt before him and for half an hour sang a long hymn, and, not showing much wisdom, called upon the Holy Spirit to inspire the stubborn sinner with divine love. After delivering this parody of religion, they took their leave, promising to return the next day.

Several small buildings, like those used in Galicia by hawkers, but smaller and on wheels, were waiting on the street. One of these, fitted out like an iron oven, was placed on the sidewalk, right beside the door of the saloon. Two women, relieved regularly every hour, sat at the window of the building and took down in a book the names of the men,—brothers, relatives or acquaintances—who visited the saloon. Pity the poor man whose name was entered in that book! What sermons he would hear when he went home!

The principal group of women went to the nearest saloon. There the owner would not let them in, and so, outdoors, in spite of the bad weather and snow, standing and kneeling in turn, they prayed for his soul and in hymns called for divine favor. Several hundred persons, jeering at what was going on and urging the tavern-keeper to hold out, gazed upon the strange sight. Germans gathered in the saloon were defiantly putting down full mugs of beer, jeering, and singing coarse drinking songs in English and German. After an hour of prayers, the increasing cold drove the women from the place. But they left the guard station and two women in charge.

I did not follow them on their further excursions. I learned, however, that they returned the next day to visit the same two saloons and that they poured a couple of casks of beer on the street. Some Irish laborer came along and drank the beer as it flowed on top of the ice!

Returning home, I couldn't help reflecting on the absurdity of scenes such as I had witnessed, and I began to wonder where more harm was done to society in Europe and America, by men in their clubs and saloons, or by their wives in the shops of the milliner or modiste. Every one of the pious women of Minneapolis dressed above her station in life. The wives and daughters of workingmen had wardrobes suitable for merchants' wives and daughters, while those of the latter class appeared in silks and velvets on the dirty sidewalks of the city. Is it any wonder their men, out of despair, turned to drink?

That evening some famous apostle of free love, journeying about the United States, delivered a public lecture in Minneapolis. She spoke to a hall filled to overflowing with people of both sexes. Some applauded, even at the absurd double entendres of this Demosthenes in skirts. Many, however, were surprised that such a handsome, young, and truly learned women would speak such trash, especially as she was, personally, an exemplary wife and mother. Nothing in this country surprises me. In America there are so many things hard to understand that I would have to be in a state of wonder all the time, if I let myself.

The next day I left Minneapolis. In the newspapers I read that the crusade kept widening every day, and with ever greater success, and that other cities were following the example of Minneapolis. I often wonder whether my host gave in to the fanatics, or followed the advice of his wife. I'd like to see those pious dames in the midst of the Germans in New Ulm. Carpenters would reap a good harvest building those guard-stations at the doors of fifty-three taverns of our local capital.

III. *Plague of Grasshoppers*

Oh, my great God, that in Thy wisdom art pleased to render so burdensome this journey of ours in this vale of tears! Here, in this Far West, Thou has granted us a fruitful and spacious land, a healthful climate, pure streams, cold as the waters of my native Carpathians,—in a word, everything to tempt man to settle here and to fall in love with his new homeland. Why dost Thou every few years send down a destroyer of the fruits of our labor?

We settled here, I myself and thousands, like me, poor creatures seeking only quiet, freedom, and a crust of bread earned by honest toil. The burning heat of summer and the bitter cold of winter did not rob our muscles of their toughness. With speed worthy of the Americans we ploughed day and night and sowed even on Good Friday and Whitsuntide.

Around our homesteads flowed fields of abundant wheat in wave upon wave billowing greenish-gold in the breeze. And it was this, this wind, that drove forward a cloud of destroyers, dense as flakes of snow in the midst of a tempest, whirling above the earth in clouds and at the same time darkening the sun above three states. In a single night, an army of devouring insects covered an expanse as large as the whole of France, and the following day consumed the fruit of a farmer's labor for an entire year.

The consuming horde did not remain long on our fields. The first wind from the east turned them around toward their native Rockies.

Their seed remained, however, on the fields they had rendered bare, on our green prairie. From this there would be born, despite the fierce cold of winter and a fitful spring, billions of their descendants, to destroy the fruit of yet another year's work.

Who will describe the threat of a new disaster! Swarms of jumping insects in compact rows slowly surrounded our sown fields, eating right down to the ground a strip of young grain. Their progress, although slow, was yet so systematic that we could actually count how many days it would take them to consume the last blade from our fields.

Other swarms, more greedy, squeezed their way inside buildings and devoured everything that was not made of wood or steel. Papers and clothing, food for man and beast, all vanished before our eyes, while we were obliged to gaze upon the destruction being wrought, without being able to check the evil.

Still other swarms ate every leaf from the young trees we had set out with such expenditure of time and labor and money. Their green had just begun to transform the wilderness into a semblance of human habitation, to shelter us from the fierce blasts of winter tempests, and to give us the hope that our children would be able to rest in shade and the coolness of the forest. What became of those trees? Naked twigs.

The time came at last when the young larvae burst the skin enclosing their youthful members. Their long wings dried in time and with the first breath of south wind they were air-borne and flying beyond our fields, their dark cloud flying toward the far north.

Part of our harvest was still left. In the middle of every field a spot of flourishing grain still shone golden and we said: at least enough still remains for our own daily bread.

And then came the Fourth of July, that great national holiday. At dawn carts and carriages were already winding across the prairie. From every hut, from every tiny village, crowds of pioneers on foot and on horseback were making their way to a nearby grove, in order, all together, as one body, without regard to differences in faith, origin and speech, to celebrate the anniversary of their new homeland's birth.

In the shade of American trees we sat at simple tables, hastily improvised, and shared the food brought by the ones who could best afford it. The older people ate and drank, the younger ran about, throwing paper cannon-balls under our feet and watching with a smile to see how many times an involuntary outcry from the ladies would let them know that these harmless bombs had frightened one of the diners. Vivats in Swedish, in German, in English with the greatest variety of accents, thundered above the reports of shots.

The guests get up from the feast and a speaker, chosen by acclamation, mounts a cart that serves as speaker's platform. Whoever the speaker,—it doesn't matter—words flow from his lips without effort, for according to hallowed custom, on this particular holiday there is but a single theme: the services performed by the fathers of the country.

Recapitulating the lives of the great and holy heroes of the nation, he rehearses for old and young, listening with intense concentration, the deeds of Washington, the sufferings of his comrades from across the sea, the services and martyrdom of

Lincoln and the duties incombent on the rest of the population. Several hundred enthusiastic faces and several hundred hands thundering applause, bear witness to the fact that those listening comprehend what is being said.

Then the tops of the trees began to hum as if from a July hail storm. The speaker stopped, his listeners looked toward the sun in terror. Above their heads, from the trees, as high as the eye could gaze, small dark spots flitted. The murmur kept increasing in intensity, the spots grew larger, and the cry rose, "Grasshoppers! Grasshoppers!" The cry was so loud that for a minute it deafened even the roar of the insects' wings, as they flew in from the west.

I do not wish to call back to mind the laments and curses that poisoned the hour during which we returned from the grove to our homes. Horses, struck in the eyes by blows from the swarm, refused to pull the carts carrying us home. The prairie, green a moment before, turned a brownish color. For a dense mass of the insects had already begun seeking rest and food on its surface.

Somehow we finally reached home. Passing our fields, we could see that every blade of wheat had its full quota of the disgusting invaders. Dusk was falling, so that we could not even think of driving the creatures from the field. The next day they flew away, leaving behind not a blade of wheat. A few days later we harnessed our horses to the plough and began turning over the soil of the absolutely bare fields.

People who a year before had been well-to-do and having so much even a week ago as to ask favor from no one, were in a single day turned into beggars. Three quarters of our fellow-citizens were obliged to live out the long winter on private collections and with the help of the government. Only by selling what they had left of their starved little property would they be able to buy whatever seed they would need for next season's planting.

Such results as I have described are the consequence of this most horrible of disasters, that every eight or ten years befalls the states lying beyond the Mississippi. Pity the poor farmer who arrives here before an invasion of grasshoppers, since for two years he will have to live on a wasteland, without hope of bread for himself and his family, even without pasture for his cattle. Long years will pass before he will be able to free himself from the burden of debts and the obligations assumed in those unhappy years.

To those reading this, it would seem that the certainty of such losses ought to deter people from settling in the west. Quite the contrary. In spite of the invasions of these pests, our settlements push ever farther, houses rise ever more densely on the hilltops, houses reminiscent of Ukrainian gravemounds, scattered about the prairie. What won't the will of stout-hearted people and hard work accomplish? Today stricken to the very ground, we recover from this year's loss before the next invasion. But before the passage of a quarter of a century, the progress of civilization and the density of population will force even the greed of these insects to discontinue their visits.

It's not easy to believe, but a fact, that as the redskins and buffaloes have retreated before the advance of settlers from the east, so will the grasshoppers. Today there are still living in the state of New York old men who remember their last invasion in the Great Lakes region, and people still fairly young who beheld those brownish swarms circling around Chicago, at that time only a modest little town. Even in eastern Minnesota, a hundred miles from us, grasshoppers have not made their incursions for more than fifteen years. It is not hard to envisage the time when, our settlements having reached the Rockies and their present nests having been put to the plough, this plague of the western farmer will have been exorcised once and for all.

Before that happens, naked fields and leafless trees will darken the landscape of the prairie. We still often see the huts of families who have fled because of hunger, returning to the east, where it is more difficult to be sure to establish an independent economy, but where each year the danger of two whole seasons of fruitless labor does not threaten.

IV. *Election Shenanigans*

A few days after my return from the Black Hills, I received from the Central Committee of the Republican Party a notice asking all the villages and towns to arrange meetings for the purpose of choosing delegates to the district conventions. From the letter addressed to me and marked by the owner of the paper by which I was employed, I knew that our party was in great danger, as the newly created third party, the Anti-Monopolists,[25] under pressure from its leaders, was going to support the Democrats. And so our problem was not only to organize our party members and hold them a hundred per cent in line on the day of the elections, but also to do as much as we could to weaken the coalition hostile to us. The Republican Party in Minnesota could be saved from complete ruin and defeat only if the most popular candidates were chosen and the cleverest men sent to the convention...

The letter mentioned above entrusted to me and me alone responsibility for guiding the fate of the Republican Party in the part of the district around Sleepy Eye, west of New Ulm. Such an honor imposed on me the greater burden in that this area was inhabited principally by Germans, and was strongly Anti-Monopolist besides. I couldn't appear publicly against the latter, as I had never concealed my own Free Trade principles, learned from the works of English economists. Many of my neighbors, hearing my defense of low tariffs in private conversations, even accused me of secret support of the Anti-Monopolist Party, which until recently had been neutral, but now was hostile to the Republicans. My foreign origin did not endear me to American hearts. Also, since I knew no Swedish, I had no way of winning the Swedish vote. And my avoidance of the Germans in the past caused me to have serious doubts as to whether, in the course of a few days, I would be able to win many friends among the Teutons. Thus I could count only on such poularity as in a somewhat primitive society attaches to one having close association with the press.

I rode horseback from hut to hut, like some agent selling machinery, asking everybody, without regard to nationality or party, to come to the village convention. The Germans I persuaded by pointing out that they should come, to keep the Americans from having the greater number of votes. With the Yankees I damned the Germans, conjuring up the fear that if they allowed these to get ahead of them locally, all the county offices would soon be in Teutonic hands. The Swedes, fanatical supporters of our party, who followed blindly the word of certain leaders operating among them, I told by signs that these leaders had empowered me to count on their participation in the local convention, and on their vote. And so I was able, working it this way, to collect several hundred persons for the Republican convention.

A friend and I took pains to collect all proclamations, left at crossroads or at the doors of shops in town, inviting Democrats to their convention. My success in getting out the vote for our convention, plus my checkmating of the plans of the opposing camp, won me the respect of the leaders of our party in the state capital. "If that fellow, after only ten months in the district, knows how to control the Republican Party in his county, and to weaken the Democratic the way he did, he must possess a remarkable gift for politics," the men up there reflected, never knowing that most of the people present at our little convention had no idea up to the last minute which party summoned them to the city.

Actually, not until after the opening of the convention did I disclose to the Germans, who were Democrats, that I had not brought them together to deliberate on how to keep the money voted by the government for wiping out the grasshopper plague from falling into the hands of the Yankees, but to help us elect a delegate to the district convention. Many of the Germans at first growled at this trick, and so I spread the whisper in German:

"As a foreigner I count on you to help me equalize the influence of the Yankees in the capital. You know very well that in our villages and counties we predominate, and it is only in gatherings held in the capital that they have the upper hand. What good does it do you to have German mayors and tax collectors, if our governors and delegates do not support our nationality? As long as you keep voting Democratic, this state of affairs will not change, since the American majority will defy you and shut you out of the highest offices. Join us and I promise you that we will force the Yankees to fill these positions with a number of foreigners."

The Germans pondered a minute and then, seeing the practical good sense of my words, to a man came over to our party.

Whether they went back again to their Democratic principles on seeing a ticket bearing not a single German name, I don't know. It really didn't matter, since we had succeeded for once in bringing disorder to their camp. Never again would they possess the full confidence of their former friends, the Irish, for in politics as in war, a deserter is always looked upon as a spy.

And so, having isolated the Irish and sown dissension between them and the Germans, we weakened the Democratic Party in our district appreciably.

The local convention, called by me, not surprisingly named me a delegate to the provincial convention. The Germans voted for me as better than nothing, knowing the Americans would never permit a pure German to be elected. The Americans, believing I had the votes of both Swedes and Germans in my pocket, did not put up another candidate. The Swedes, not understanding a word of what went on at our local convention, supported everything I said, in this following the nod of their leaders. This was enough to assure them that the representative from their county would vote in harmony with their principles.

V. *Convention Trickery*

Our district, consisting of four counties, sent four delegates to the voting convention, each and every one elected, I assure you, by the same kind of shenanigans as I have described in ours.

On arriving at the capital of our district, we discovered that one county, and that my own, had failed to choose a delegate to the Democratic Convention. We learned this from the fact that in the best hotel in town four Republicans and three Democrats, all delegates to the convention, were spending the night.

The two conventions were to take place in Shakopee, five hours by train from New Ulm, where we were. The Democratic was to be held the very next day, ours the day after.

What were we to do to keep those Democrats from reaching their goal? I pondered the problem.

And so what I did was take those three fellows down to the beer hall in the hotel and, sparing no money, give them a good send-off for their journey. The three were all Germans, and I entertained them not only with beer, but with tales of Australia and Europe, as long as they would listen. Finally one of them came to and said, "We must get to bed. Get some sleep. Remember, the train goes at six in the morning."

"Boots!" another of the Democrats called, "Don't forget to wake us up tomorrow before daylight."

With these words the three proceeded to the bedroom assigned them by the proprietor.

Now in American hotels, the fellow they call Boots fulfills the function not only of boot-and-garment cleaner, but of waker-upper as well. And so, after the Germans had gone, I spoke to him as he was marking their room-number on the soles of their shoes.

"What's your name, Boots?" I inquired.

"Gustav Winy."

"Where are you from?"

"From Sweden."

"You speak good English."

(God forgive me for this: his English was execrable.)

"I have a natural gift for languages and though I've been here only six months, I speak the language of the people here pretty good," Boots replied, obviously pleased with my compliment.

"And so you've been here only half a year? I don't suppose you've mixed into politics. You probably don't know our division into parties?"

"I haven't voted yet, but already I've got my citizenship papers, and I'll vote at the next elections."

"And what party will you join?"

"We Swedes are always Republicans. That's because the Irish belong to the other party."

"What have you got against the Irish?"

"They compete with us for jobs on the railroads that are being built. In the old days only an Irishman could get a job on the railroad, and it hasn't been long that they've been hiring our people."

"Boots," I said, with the voice of a gravedigger, "did you notice who those three gentlemen are in the big room upstairs?"

"Germans."

"Worse than that! They're Democrats, going to the convention in Shakopee."

Boots opened his gray eyes wide and scratched his blond head.

"Democrats!" he shouted, in a rage.

"Yes, Democrats!" I said, bitterly. "And if they don't oversleep so that they miss their train, the fault will be yours that they get to Shakopee in time."

"But I can't MAKE them oversleep!"

"Don't wake them up, Boots, just don't wake them up! Anybody that has drunk twenty mugs of beer won't be waking up at six in the morning if Boots doesn't knock on their door."

"How can I be sure the gentlemen are really Democrats?"

"Just wait a few minutes and I'll prove it to you."

I grabbed my hat and hurried to the home of a certain Mr. Rukke, an educated Swede, in charge of the office of District Vice-Treasurer. In the pocket of this man reposes the voting record of every Swede in the district.

I got Rukke out of bed and brought him to the hotel. My idea pleased him so much that he not only encouraged his fellow-countryman not to waken the Democrats, but ordered him not to. The proprietor of the hotel, sharing our principles to the full, also praised my stratagem.

Leaving Boots and several bystanders on guard, so as not to take a chance on other guests or some servant waking the delegates before dawn, we went to the railroad station ourselves around five. Our opponents were not on hand, and, as it turned out, slept right through until eight. The traitor Boots not only did not waken them, but closed the window blinds so carefully and kept everybody in the hotel so quiet that even after the delegates woke up, they couldn't believe the evidence of their watches.

Naturally, the next day the telegraph lines hummed with the news that the Democratic Party was so disorganized in New Ulm that they didn't send even a single delegate to the convention. The word was carried not only to the state capital, but to Washington. You have to live in the West and be plunged in party fanaticism in order to understand how much that tiny incident delighted our friends and enraged our opponents. In view of the balance existing between the two parties and the importance of the present conflict, the defection of a single county has its significance and exerts a moral influence. It took only one modest Boots to tip the scale, in an electoral district numbering two hundred thousand inhabitants, to the side of one of the many candidates.

Arriving in Shakopee, we went straight to the Democratic convention, not in order to vote, but to help with the intrigues carried on by our supporters, to break up the coalition of the Anti-Monopolists[25] with the Democrats. The problem was made easier by the fact that the Germans and the Irish hated each other mutually, and the ones directing each party yearned to rule the whole camp. As with all coalitions of whatever kind, so with this: premature death threatened it because of the ambition of the leaders.

> [With the aid of money supplied by the party, Wiśniowski was able to set delegate against delegate, on the basis of nationality, and, when balloting began, to be pretty certain his candidate would win.]

Just as the announcement of winner was about to be made, a noise was heard at the door, and three figures, all out of breath, pushed into the hall. They were none other than the three delegates from New Ulm! The three men, having arrived by the afternoon train, had come on a running trot to the hall. Their appearance changed the whole aspect of the situation. The opponents of our candidate took courage and decreed that a new vote should be taken. I felt sure that if this happened, forty-seven votes would be cast against our candidate and he would lose.

And so I turned to the fellow standing beside me, an old farmer from some wild part of the region, from whose appearance and uncouth manner I knew that he paid little attention to social forms. He was the typical pioneer-politician, in boots up to his knees, in a coat hanging like a bag, a hat with a patch on one side and a considerable hole on the other, from which a few unhappy locks of hair stuck up, like the spines on a snake. This delegate vowed eternal friendship over three bottles of wine, provided at my expense on behalf of the public good.

"And why don't you protest this new counting of votes?" I asked him. "Why, the convention was called to order a long time ago. And these three gentlemen haven't the right to be seated in it until they show their authorization."

Stirred up by me, the farmer bawled out a solemn protest against accepting the new delegates into the bosom of the convention. The presiding officer, not knowing what to do, demanded of the three, in order to show his authority, papers signed by the presidents and secretaries of the county conventions, something official that would show they had been elected according to legal forms.

"Unfortunately," the newcomers cried, "we have no papers whatsoever with us. The servant at the hotel not only did not waken us in time, as ordered, but he also lost our valise at the railroad station. We ordered him to send it to Shakopee, and he sent it to St. Paul. Our authorizations are all travelling in that valise. However, we can call the newspapers and friends here who know very well that we are not demanding anything that does not belong to us, and we beg for recognition of the rights properly owing us."

"I protest the admission to the convention of persons not accredited to it!" cried my pioneer-friend in the hat full of holes.

The president was by this time twisting and turning as if he were sitting on pins and needles. So he decided to cut the Gordian knot in a manner highly amusing.

"I put it to the judgment of the convention whether these gentlemen have a right to vote or not. Whoever is in favor, say 'Aye.'"

"Aye," cried more than forty voices.

"Whoever is against, say 'No.'"

"No!" sang the choir of some forty voices.

"A tie," the president went on, "and so let the gentlemen delegates divide into two camps. All those saying 'Aye' stand on the right, those saying 'No' on the left."

The division into two groups, hating each other equally, went on amid noise, confusion and smiles. Forty-five delegates stood on the left side, forty-four on the right, and the three newcomers stood in the middle of the hall.

"The 'Nos' have it!" cried the president. "The gentlemen who have just arrived will be good enough to leave the convention."

VI. *Turning the Tide in Winona*

Most of the Winonans of the Roman Catholic faith regarded it as a kind of religious duty to vote the Democratic ticket, trained by the injunctions of the bishop, more often than not, to regard as a traitor anyone daring to revolt openly against their politically minded priests. How dangerous for a free country must be the blind obedience of half the population to its theocracy of whatever party, we see in the last elections, wherein the barbarous plantation owners of the South and the political scoundrels of New York were again elected lords of the republic.

Summoned by Mr. Dunnell, the Republican candidate for Congress in the district of Winona, I changed my personal life and plans in order to see to it that this community not choose an ally so unflattering to Poles. Having provided myself with funds for the purpose, on a certain Saturday I boarded a certain car in New Ulm and after a half day's journey found myself at the banks of the Mississippi. With my bag in hand I hurried toward the quarter of Winona known as Poland and got a room in a hostel where, from owner to boy, only the Mazurian dialect was spoken. Well nourished with *zrazy*[26] and cucumber pickles, after a long conversation with Maciej and Kaska, I went to bed and dreamed of home.

The church bell woke me from pleasant dreams. With astonishment I saw that the sun had flooded my room with its rays. Dressing as quickly as I could, I hurried to a red brick church with wooden spire.

This house of God, the most tasteful and spacious in Winona, was built at a cost of many thousands of dollars, collected from free-will offerings. A gracious and ample rectory and school next door completed a pleasant impression.

A large congregation occupied the benches and chairs of the church. The men were sitting on the right, women on the left. Neat clothes, always spotlessly clean, convinced me that my fellow-countrymen in Winona had already adopted the dress of the American working man. Still, more than one old country coat and cap of transatlantic cut pleasingly modified the uniformity of black overcoats and silk dresses, and testified to the fact that the older generation clings to the clothing they brought with them from Europe as to a reliquary.

The music, remembered from childhood, and the Latin liturgy, transported me into a kind of hypnosis. So also did the garb of the priest, with his head gray as a dove, the heads of the worshippers, bowing in humility, and the sermon, delivered in a tongue almost never heard. Politics and half-American customs and religious views that had become a part of me,—all these fled at once from my mind. In the company of these children I too became a child. I humbled myself and drank in the words of the liturgy and the teachings of the sermon. The elderly priest instructed his flock in a manner not too involved nor above their understanding, and it was not for me to criticize, as the entire community listened attentively to his message.

It was not until after the sermon and following the completion of the Mass that I received a most unpleasant impression. Father J..., the seventy year old pastor of Winona, launched into a kind of political oration, the less bearable on my part as this was not the place for such a speech, and since the one delivering it betrayed the most profound lack of understanding as to conditions in the country where he was living, and in which he was supposed to instruct his sheep. In delivering his most telling arguments either against a candidate or on his behalf, whether he condemned such a one or lauded him, the preacher based his appeal on the bishop.

And so, bored by the stupid talk and reacting against its being delivered here in any case, I left the church, inflexibly determined to checkmate the designs of the reverend pastor.

I am not going to catalog the means I took to accomplish this end, not wishing to reveal too faithful a description of the election quirks used in America. Whatever I could do by mere talking, by advice, persuasion and flattery with persons having some sort of influence, that I did in Winona. The departure of Father J... for Chicago in a couple of days made my task easier. When he returned he was astounded to find a Polish Republican Committee actively working in opposition to the Democratic Committee. And when at the general meeting of the people of Winona almost all the Poles voted for delegates indicated by me, he was even more taken aback.

WISCONSIN, THE NEW POLAND

This chapter is to be found in *Koronacja króla Fidżi*, 352-54.

THE NEW POLAND: WISCONSIN

If you look up the word *dalles* in a French dictionary, you will find, instead of a single Polish word, a description of the formation: "a narrow river channel between high, rocky walls."

In the fir forests of Wisconsin you will hear the term, transformed into the English word Dells, and you can prepare yourself for a soul-stirring sight, as The Dells have provided here, in one of the most beautiful of the American states, a remarkable phenomenon...

On its northern border Wisconsin has the blue waters of Lake Superior, on its eastern the yellow current of Lake Michigan, and on the west the green tide of the upper Mississippi.

Of all the places in the world I have visited, Wisconsin reminds me more affectionately than any other of my native land: in its geological formations, its superficial contours, pine forests, and especially in its climate, which is completely identical with ours. Even more does it resemble my own homeland in the tuneful sound of its precious speech, which you hear more often than anywhere else in America throughout the hamlets of this state.

Not forgetting Milwaukee, the capital of the state, with its Polish church that cost fifty thousand dollars and its parish of five thousand souls, you could make a pleasureable pilgrimage from the city of Green Bay, with its numerous Silesian colony, across the state to Winona on the Mississippi, where you will find, of the eleven thousand inhabitants there, at least thirty-five hundred Kashubians. Going south from Green Bay on an inlet of Lake Michigan in the east, you pass through Manitowoc, right on the lake. Here you will find a Polish community and church, also farms scattered among the pinewoods and prairie. You will come upon small towns as neat and clean as Berlin with a half dozen houses bearing the sign in Polish, "Good Beer Here." Also a Cloister of Poor Clares and more than one rectory.

A little to the north and east of Winona, you arrive at a settlement with the romantic name Arcadia. Here my friends so occupy themselves in litigation that they urged me to stay forever, to help them out, for here, they complained, "these American lawyers are a poor lot. They'll skin you alive, and no one knows how to speak to the Judge, not even our high-mucky-muck."

Going on a little farther, you come to Pine Creek, surrounding a small church, coquettishly building, and ten farmhouses. Now at last you draw up to the crystal current of the Father of Waters, the Mississippi.

During the course of this whole journey I have described, you could stop almost every night at a cottage where you would be greeted with the salutation, "Niech będzie pochwalony..." It might be a rectory, or a small farmhouse already displaying a bright coat of paint, as if to say, "Yes, God has indeed blessed us." Or it might be a log-and-sod hut, in which some poor settler is beginning the struggle with northern Nature. Whatever it is, you will see out front a tow-headed little girl, born in America, often so far Germanized or Americanized as only to lisp a bit in the tongue of her parents. Even the dogs here, like foxes and of no special breed, somehow bark in a fashion of their own. And often, intermingled with the chatter of the little girl and the racket made by the hoarse-throated dogs, you will hear the murmur of those falls I have spoken of, these *dalles*, blown to your ears by the wind.

It was not advertisements that lured these pioneers to this place. No adventurer, whose family came from the Crimea, conceived an idea of founding here a New Radom or Kalisz or Częstochowa, or of selling wasteland to people enticed from across the sea. No fever consumes the children of these settlers, as too often seems to be the case in settlements loudly advertised.

No, the thousands and thousands of people who years ago founded a settlement above the *dalles* of Wisconsin came here of their own will, in response to an offer from Uncle Sam of land, to be given free, in the vicinity of forests and close to navigable rivers. Today it is only in Oregon, and perhaps not even there, that you can find such an offer.

And so the people settled on this land that they had been given. In the forests deer were to be found, and in the rivers abundant fish. And so, although fifteen years ago they had to wear bast sandals for shoes, and to live like children of the wild on fish and corn, these settlers had only to wait for the day when for every acre once received as a gift, they were able to realize several tens of dollars. The burgeoning state of these people today impels me to discourse at greater length on a country full of tender memories and romantic scenes, and populated by so many people who speak my own tongue... [27]

LANGENOR

[A Tale of Love, Loneliness and Longing

in the American West]

Motto:

Beware the maid, my little son,
The maid beware, O darling one...
—Heine

CHAPTER ONE

The Hermit of the Montana Wilderness

For a long time I wondered what it was that made Langenor embrace the wilderness, why he drove himself, of his own free will and systematically, to efface all traces of what must have been an excellent bringing up. Why he tried to cover with a veil of crudity and coarseness treasures of learning and feeling brought from his homeland. Where he came from and what his real name was, I finally found out, not without difficulty. Where he is now, I do not know, since the paths of our lives took opposite directions, and I lost sight of him. Lands and seas divided us and kept us apart, but even more were we separated by something else: difference of station. Already I have ceased to wander with him among the defiles and on the slopes of the Black Hills, and no more shall I be bivouacing in his company in the wilds of Montana. But neither I, nor any tourist, adventurer, officer or scholar who received his hospitality will ever forget that lanky, vigorous hermit.

As for me, I find him to be the prime example, the typical representative of the small group of those eccentrics who, in love with wandering and far from home, lead a life their stay-at-home brothers can never understand. And so I give him to you as the first in a series of portraits from Polish-American life. I make bold to exploit this field beyond the ocean on which dwell more than a hundred thousand of our brothers, in order, by my pioneer labors, to attract pens far more clever than mine to the rich stores inherent in that new scene of our activities.

Langenor had two callings.

In summer he was a squatter, pasturing and caring for his flocks, in winter a trapper, capturing in steel traps animals valuable for their fur. For diversion he hunted with firearms, or fished, or panned for gold in the streams of Montana.

For the country and times in which he lived, Langenor was well off. In summer he lived in a deep ravine or canyon beyond a hunting ground of fir trees, near a waterfall, far from the haunts and trails of white men. In winter he lived in the town of Helena, at the foot of the mountains.

So preoccupied was Langenor with his own affairs, that, in the custom of the West which honors business above all, he would often greet a guest the minute he met him with such a question as, "How much is meat selling for in Helena, or fur in Virginia City?" The people of Montana are not given to wordiness, but they anger easily and like to swear. Langenor would get angry, like the rest, but his fury was like a flash flood in the mountains, over in the twinkling of an eye. His lips, generally swollen with pride, were delicate as a maiden's, and his smile revealed a good-hearted nature. On meeting a guest his bright eyes would rest for a moment on him, as he sized him up morally and physically. He would run his fingers through his thick, curly hair, and, if satisfied, would invite you to his hut, where he treated you with all the hospitality of those whose first principle is, "czym chata bogata tem rada."[28]

In Helena it was whispered that as a boy Langenor went to the best schools, schools of such high standing that no miner understood how to say their name. His closest neighbor during the summer season in the wild lived in another canyon four hours distant, and he was one of those responsible for spreading this opinion. He based his view on the fact that a year ago, when some German came through the mountains on a collecting trip for Uncle Sam, Langenor had an altercation with him at their very first meeting. The learned doctor seized a firebrand that was only half burned and with it began marking the trunk of the nearest birch tree with strange cyphers, also with Roman letters and the word *log*. But this was not the whole of it, since often the doctor looked at the sun when it stood at the top of the sky, through a strange instrument. What he was interested in was the exact geographic location of the place in which they stood.

Langenor also began making marks on his side of the birch tree, but with his bowie knife, in the sand. Finally he outtalked the doctor, making him so angry that with his fag-end he hit Langenor over the hand. Those looking on saw a duel in the making over those mashed fingers, with themselves as seconds.

But the whole thing ended finally with only a broken pair of glasses.

The affair with the "collecting doctor" afforded one bit of evidence as to Langenor's being an educated man, but there was also the affair of the Mexican Jesuits, who came through the mountains on one of their missions. Though knowing no Spanish, Langenor was able to carry on a conversation with the priest,— in Latin, naturally.

Langenor's little homestead in the canyon consisted of a stockade surrounded by palisades fifteen feet high. The palisades formed a girdle about a deep ditch. In the center of the stockade stood a hut fashioned of round logs, set up on a foundation of rough rocks, joined together without mortar. The cracks between the rocks were chinked with dried moss. In the center of the hut stood an iron stove, a huge one, and on the top of this, three feet above his head, Langenor warmed his feet whenever he was at home. His fondness for this position plus other eccentricities confirmed Langenor's neighbors in their conviction that he was a native American, or that he had come to America as a young child. He did, however, speak with a slight accent, a certain hesitancy or stammering, especially when he was under the influence of powerful emotions. It was as if he could not think of the word he wanted that quickly. This marked him as different from his northern neighbors, but they thought no more of it than that he might have come from the southern part of Texas, and was probably born there.

Langenor's stove stood on the exact point on which government surveyors sometimes place their turret, exactly where certain degrees of latitude and longitude cross. Langenor chose this point for the center of his hut, stockade and claim, saying that if ever a town were founded there, his location would not have to be surveyed further.

Langenor's fame extended beyond Helena, Virginia City, and the borders of Montana. Once he had distinguished himself in war with the Indians, so that even in Washington he was known. Montana was grateful to him for "relieving them"— that was what breaking a neck was called in this courteous society—of a well-known hoodlum by the name of Bailey. This cavalier of revolver and sabre paid for food and drink with bullets, enticed the miners to play against him, raked in their money, lost and won. Meeting Langenor, he actually forced him to play. From his modesty, quiet manner, and the way he would rub his head in thought, the hooligan took Langenor for a lamb.

Bailey had the reputation of being a sharp judge of people, but obviously he was not. Having lost in a game with Langenor, not only did he not want to pay, but he gave the squatter a sharp blow on the nose. That was too much for Langenor's patience. Grabbing the hooligan's two arms in his own right arm, which was harder than a miner's tongs, he fixed it so that Bailey could not grab his gun. Then he beat him with the handle of his hunting whip. Finally Bailey managed to free himself, took a shot at Langenor, but missed. With this the tall Langenor seized his revolver from Bailey's hand and with the handle of the hooligan's own weapon, broke the bandit's skull.

After this encounter Langenor did not have to worry about intruders. He lived in peace, with the respect of all. He was called upon to act as judge in all affairs of honor, and pale-faced bullies, yes, even Indian plunderers, passed his stockade without disturbing him, and the trails leading to his home were thenceforth safe.

Yet in all this, Langenor was not a happy man. As he confessed to me with his own lips, while guiding me across the range separating the sources of the Missouri, whose waters eventually reach the Gulf of Mexico, and those of the Columbia River, which flows into the Pacific Ocean. The whole cause of the man's melancholy was just one thing: woman. Or rather, lack of a woman.

We spread our tent, and soon a fire was crackling. Resting our heads on a log, we lay in complete happiness, the kind one enjoys only after consuming a savory stag, roasted over the coals, and when, after a hard day, one has a pillow under one's head, even if it is not a soft one. We had travelled eight geographic miles that day, over hills, through defiles, and now we were stopping, as they say in the West, on the soil of No Man's

Land. By right of first seizure, everything around us that we wished to take belonged to us.

A crystal-pure cascade murmured nearby. With its foam it spattered the alpine anemones and descended into islands of trees, leaving the air full of the tinkle of some wild melody. Except for this wild murmur of the waters, there was nothing to break the utter silence of the pinewood save the cry of an owl, frightened away by the arc of our campfire.

Langenor sighed. Not an ordinary sigh, but one that sounded, with its apologetic note, more like the cry of a coyote than what might come from a human breast.

"What's so bad?" I asked. "What makes you groan that way? Are you sick?"

"No. Just then a sad thought flew through my head."

"About your stockade, perhaps? Don't worry yourself about that. Your cattle have got enough to eat. They won't start getting thin before you get back. That red shieldbearer of yours will guard them and give them food."

"And probably sleep right through, the rascal, and not feed them for three days. But it wasn't my property I was thinking of."

"Then was it what Dickens calls some 'skeleton in the closet' ?"

"Dickens was talking about family skeletons."

"But he knew also that every one of us carries in his heart some skeleton of his own. Memories of things lost, that we can't recover. Repentance for something we can not confess. Regret that what has happened is over and done, and can't be changed."

"You're right. And that skeleton we carry with us even into this lonely place. And even here we find no happiness, though we have left that phantom a long, long way behind us."

"There's no use searching for it anywhere, since it really

dwells in our own selves. But what do you lack for happiness,—the kind you like—that the wilderness can not give?"

"Well, I have a fine herd of cattle, a claim, and a homestead of my own in the mountains. I have a hut in the city. On my farm I've fitted up my house with a small sofa, a chest of drawers, even a folding screen with Japanese flowers, the only one in the country, to divide the place into two rooms, one for living, one for sleeping. In the bank in Virginia City there's a good round sum in my name. But what's all that—nothing."

Here Langenor ran his fingers more busily than ever through his hair.

"Hmm. If you only had some purpose in life, or some person who could enjoy all this with you. A companion, someone to keep house for you. A wife, even. Well, you wouldn't be so depressed, would you?"

"You have it right," the hermit said without hesitation, seemingly glad that I had supplied him with the logical conclusion to his words. "But when you come to that, it's out of the question."

Obviously wishing to console himself for the unhappy memories his heartfelt confession had called up, Langenor took from a small bag fastened to his belt a cake of prime tobacco. He cut off a good-size slice and began to chew it.

I had to say something.

"Come now," I began. "In Helena I know a dozen young women, and there isn't one of them would deny you her hand. Take a chance. Buck up, have courage. You misanthropes, you challenge an old mother-bear singlehanded, but you let the words suitable for speaking in the presence of a young girl stick in your throat. When we get back to Helena in the fall, I'll be your matchmaker."

"It's no use," Langenor said. "I have no luck with women."

"That again? With your reputation, fortune, position?"

Langenor raised his hand to brush aside my compliments.

"All for nothing," he said. "Here in the mountains girls are scarcer than angel visitors. In Helena I know a few. But either too young, or with too western manners. There are some who might be suitable for me, but the minute I get near one, they call up recollections and comparisons that spoil it all. A companion, I do need. It's time I established regular habits. So many times I've moved! I began farming in the south, in Texas. Now here I am in northern Montana. I can't go any farther. I'd settle in Canada, but I don't like their European government. As for a helpmate,—there hasn't been one, and there won't be."

"The trouble with you is, you've never really made a sincere search."

"You think so? Just listen to this."

CHAPTER TWO

C manche Bride

For a while Langenor said nothing, busying himself with various tasks. He seized his axe and began cutting branches, then split a log and made the chips fly, as he wielded his cutting instrument with long, wide swings of his arm.

Then he sat down beside me and began. This is the story he told me.

—Eight years ago I was on the Texas border, very young at the time, but also very down-hearted, because of the loss of what I regarded as my life's greatest treasure.

In my despair, I gave up home, profession, everything, and plunged into the wilderness. My head was full of the romance of pioneer life, an illusion from which I was quickly cured. I was dreaming of red-skinned heroines and kindly Indian maidens, of flaming glances, responding willingly to the language of adoring eyes. I was under the illusion that these maidens do not pretend, that they do not compel absurd vows, do not repulse a friend though he is young and before he is able to establish himself. Do not force him to confess that he is giving himself to another admirer. I decided to find among the Indians a helpmate, to live by hunting and to forget the one I had lost.

A year after my arrival on the frontier there appeared what seemed like an opportunity to realize my heart's desire. A General, preparing for a military and scientific expedition into New Mexico, recognized in me a sharp eye, cold blood, ability to endure thirst, and a talent for the wilderness trail. He accepted me for training as a guide. It wasn't long before I outstripped my teacher. No one knew better than I the trails made by man, the signs that water was near. I was paid handsomely and right then and there started the habit of saving which was to become the foundation of my fortune.

One day we set up our tents on the border of Comanche territory. The most famous of their chieftains paid us a formal visit. In his retinue were half a dozen braves, his wives, and one daughter.

The daughter struck me as the very ideal of Indian charm, a model of womanliness, though she was but fourteen years of age. Actually, in this nation and climate a maiden develops very youn . She could have sat as a sculptor's model, had one wished to fashion an Indian Venus.

She was of medium stature, like the Florentine Venus in Rome. She had a supple and slender waist, developed, rounded, and her elkskin jacket concealed no movement whatsoever of her charming figure. The jacket reached to her knees and was embroidered all over with the spines of a snake, and at the bottom were fringes of one skin and little silver bells. Tight-fitting mocassins and gaiters adorned her small, well-formed legs and feet. The bronze tint of her neck, the darkness of her face, added to her charm in my eyes. Regular features, full lips, plus an expression sometimes sad, sometimes flirtatious, made up for lack of a white breast. Coal-black, shining braids hung loose and low, the part in her hair outlined with carmine. On her brow was fastened a massive silver buckle of Spanish workmanship.

The Indian girl knew very well that she had made an impression on me, and responded to my burning glances with a thousand gracious gestures. Race had nothing to do with the case: all these signs had the appearance and source which showed them to be the first principles of the art of coquetry. We couldn't exchange a single word with each other, but words were not necessary. I followed the circle of the Indian campfire to pursue the shape of her shadow. I thought nothing of hunger, of duty. I returned to my tent only when the Indians retired to their tepees, fashioned of skin, in order to rest. All night long I dreamed of paradise, and at dawn was again in the camp of the Comanches.

The girl's father received me graciously, though he knew what was up, and so the courting went smoothly, as far as he was concerned.

But what about the feelings of the daughter? For you see that while Indian maidens appear to have no will of their own in choosing a husband, this is really not the case at all. The father sells you a young squaw and you take her from his wigwam to your tent or hut. But if you take her against her will, you are brewing yourself a whole pot of trouble. The maiden will sulk, bite, throw herself on you with a knife, hide away, malinger, and after a few days will flee back o her father, at worst, with some other lover. Your only satisfaction in such a case will be in getting back the sum you have paid her father for the girl.

I did not try to take the Comanche girl against her will. Knowing the customs and artifices of the Indians, I decided to test her feelings that very evening. There was no lack of rivals for her hand, since every brave in her father's retinue was after her. I entered into competition with them and in accordance with Indian regulations each of us had to prove his case: to whom the beautiful maiden was attracted, and with whom, of her own free will, she would go, leaving her father's wigwam.

At dusk I said farewell to her family and withdrew a little way from the campfire. I hid in the high grass of the prairie, but in such a way as to let them know I was on guard. I was aware that several of the young braves were doing exactly the same thing I was. The rivals waited, hoping for the moment when her figure would appear in the half-light of the starlit night.

When her father left the scene, so that he could not see her, she slipped out of camp and began with a show of indifference to gather fuel for the fire. For a while she roved about on the prairie. The tawny admirer closest to where she was gave a leap...took hold of her, lifted her up. Against the backdrop of the evening sky the athletic figure of that conqueror was etched. But the maiden gave a cry and freed herself from his arms. She leapt to one side and with the fleetness of a fawn sped across the field. The brave did not pursue her. We understood that it was not he whom she sought. Accepting defeat with utter passivity, he returned to his campfire and began to smoke his pipe.

The second suitor fared no better. Finally the girl came close to my own hiding place. I put out an arm for her and carried her along the bed of a dry stream. We sat together beneath an overhanging bank. No one pursued us. No one came running after us. Indians have their own etiquette in these matters and are strict in observing them. I threw my cloak over our two heads and shoulders. She made no protest. Patiently she accepted my first kiss. At later ones she displayed no anger. I had won her in strict accordance with all the Indian rules of courtship. We returned to the campfire, hands locked together.

The next day I proceeded to the Comanche camp in dress uniform, accompanied by an interpreter, as I did not know a word of the Comanche tongue. My interpreter Caballero, half-Mexican, half-Indian, a foxy one, very cunning in matters of this sort, warned me harshly not to betray impatience, or by word or gesture show any inclination to bargain for my beloved. Later he explained to me just how he negotiated the purchase of a wife.

"This young man," he said to the chieftain, who was all on fire for the deal, while he himself struck a pose of indifference, "this young man is anxious to free you from a parasite. Your daughter is ugly as a buffalo, lazy as a brown bear and unwilling to do any hard work. The girl doesn't know how to eat or cook, is a worry to her mother and a burden on you. All the Comanche squaws laugh at her untidiness. This young man is sorry for you and will take her to his mother, to teach her. Out of pure friendship for you he will do this. He swears that he does it for you, not out of yearning for her."

"What?" the chieftain cried, with a blaze of fury that would assure a newcomer to the provincial stage unquestioned triumph. "What? You want to take my little plaything, my dearest darling daughter, the loveliest, the tenderest, the most diligent daughter a warrior ever possessed? The best cook, the most skilled in tearing skins from the buffalo, the most adept in the stringing of beads and the sewing of jackets? No. Never will I give up my darling to anyone, especially to this white youth of yours. He is still too young. His mother will beat my darling. And besides, who is he, what has he ever done to make a name for himself? Has he ever taken a single scalp? Ever stolen a single horse? Such arts as these he has never learned. He will carry her off, far from the land of the Comanches. No, I'll never give her up, even if he pays me twenty ponies."

"Twenty, you say, twenty ponies?" The interpreter rose to the word, putting on an air of astonishment. "Twenty ponies? Has the chief of a great nation become such a stupid fool? Twenty ponies for an ugly, lazy girl who's not worth a single buffalo skin? The maidens I could buy from the Pawnees for my young white friend for that price! I'll give you two ponies."

"Go to the Pawnees, then! Pawnees,—umph!" the chieftain grunted in disgust. "Twenty ponies, and that's it."

"Stupid chief of the Comanches! Even his old wife wouldn't be so shameless!"

And so the two began to have it back and forth in this spirit until wise men, not familiar with the course of Indian bargaining, would have thought it was going to come to blows between the two. Actually there was no danger. An exchange of insults was the indispensable condition of a deal involving a redskin wife. The father was expected to praise the wares he had for sale, the interpreter to demean them.

The old man came down gradually five, six, eight ponies, stopping at ten because he knew I wanted the maiden and could pay if I had to. If he had known I had no mother-cook, he would have made the price higher, but the interpreter did not let him know this, and kept reminding him of my mother. In the end the chief accepted eight ponies and two crimson blankets. In addition he warned me not to let my mother beat the girl with either a whip or a twig.

The wedding was set for the following day, the ceremony being strictly according to Indian custom, which consisted simply of the girl being led from the tepee of the Comanches to my tent. In honor of the ceremony the General presented the Indians with an ox. They led the beast along the bed of the very dry stream where the day before I had won the girl's tender heart, and profiting from the occasion I planted a thousand kisses on the burning lips of the Indian beauty.

Our love-making was interrupted by an emissary from the girl's father. He summoned her to the stream in order to help remove the skin from the ox. I was bored without her presence and so it was not long before I too hurried to the bed of the stream. Out of the place in which yesterday I had fondled my love, they had made a shambles. She sat there disembowelling the ox. She would plunge her round arms deep into the interior of the beast and then pull them up, dripping with gore and warm fat that she would offer to the whole company. Her companions gulped it down greedily, as if it were an Indian specialty. My betrothed greeted me with a smile, as she put a warm, raw bite to her lips, and swallowed it almost without chewing at all. Her eyes glistened with pleasure, as if she were eating caramels.

I turned on my heel after a single look at what was going on and in five minutes was standing in front of my General.

"General," I blurted, "I understand that tonight you are sending emissaries to Fort Lyon. It's a long journey, over territory full of Apaches, and every other kind of Indian devils. I hear you haven't been able to find volunteers. General! Let me go on this expedition!"

"You? Now? What's happened? What about the girl?"

"General! Let me go. In ten minutes I'll be ready."

"Go—go to the devil with you, and a hundred of them. Get out. Go. Saddle up and be off. They'll scalp you alive for this, those fellows, if they ever get their hands on you."

I saddled my horse and was off. Never since that day have I laid eyes on that chief, his daughter, or the ponies I paid for her. But, you know how it is,—fire goes out. And now for us. The stars up there tell me it's about midnight. Tomorrow we've got to be up at dawn to cross the ice before the sun starts to soften it. Tomorrow night when we make camp I'll tell you another adventure like this one. See how the stars glitter and twinkle among the branches and pine-boughs. You've spent time in many countries of the world: tell me, have you ever seen the stars looking so bright, so cold, and so far away as from a peak of the Rocky Mountains?—

Before I could get out an answer, I was sound asleep.

CHAPTER THREE

The Faithless Cheyenne

Once again we had a campfire merrily burning. Huge tongues of flame swirled above the top of our tent, which shone red in their glow. They licked the needles of the pine trees, which crackled and curled as they felt the touch of the hellish foe. Outside our tent a magnificent cascade murmured and roared. Tresses of water shot up like flashes of lightning, sheaves of water glistened with the fire of diamonds. Clouds of vapor burned in the arc of our fire, like fountains of flame cast heavenward from the breast of Vulcan....

Opposite us, beyond a deep ravine, rose a series of mountains, in the form of unmeasured amphitheatres, tier on tier, one above the other. Only Nature knows how to build edifices such as these. The lowest terrace was drowned in mist, the black pines growing on it shutting out the light. Above, the higher contours were more clearly outlined: bare, granite slopes reflecting the half-light of the full moon. Here and there rose from the mouth of the ravine great clumps of trees that swayed in the breeze like huge ostrich plumes, adorning steel helmets. Above all this magnificence, like a candlestick of utterly vast proportions, flamed an ice-formation whose arms widespread as in a cross resembled the shape of the Holy Tree to such an extent as to give the very name to the whole range of mountains: The Holy Cross Range. Around the ice-formation rises the cupola of The Mountain of the Holy Cross itself,[29] lofty, gigantic, menacingly beautiful, a throne fashioned of silver and worthy of the very monarch of our earthly universe, an alabaster column supporting the firmament. About this, despite the full moon, were to be seen those swarms of stars, uncounted numbers of them, which Langenor says twinkle more briskly and seem to be farther away in these parts than anywhere else in the world. Tonight, my companion averred, the stars shone too brightly, a foreboding of storm.

In front of our campfire, just ahead of us, appeared a forbidding black precipice, in the depths of this an abyss that wound in long perspective westward. From the heart of the abyss rose the roar of a great river whose waters would eventually reach the Pacific Ocean. We were camped, you can see, on a tributary of the Columbia River, on the height separated from the Holy Cross Mountains by a defile closed in by vertical, impenetrable walls. We had reached the final objective of our excursion. Seeing the mountains across the river, and the frightening abyss at their base, we had fulfilled our purpose in coming here. Tomorrow we would get ready for the return journey to Langenor's stockade.

My companion, in keeping with his promise to tell me more of his adventures with women, was ready to go on. As a slight frost made the air penetratingly cold so far up in the mountains, even though it was only June, we lay down with out feet toward the fire, wrapped ourselves well in our blankets, and spread a buffalo hide over our knees. Thus protected against the night chill, I listened to Lanenor's story:

—After my adventure with the Comanches, I never returned to New Mexico or Texas, but settled in the foothills of the Rockies, in what was then western Kansas and is today Colorado. Hordes of adventurers were crowding into that area in those days, to the streams and gold-bearing ravines at the foot of Pike's Peak. As a guide, and contractor for buffaloes and stags for these inexperienced newcomers, I collected a golden harvest. I often visited the country of the Cheyennes, which was full of animal life. This particular Indian tribe was considered to be the most restless and hostile of all, but by treating them carefully I was able to cajole these brigands and cutthroats into giving me permission to hunt in their country, and even to build a stockade close to their village. No other white man had ever enjoyed this privilege.

A year of living close to these people had wiped out my prejudices, even the feeling I had had against eating suet and grease fresh from the carcass of an animal. Probably by this time I would not even have spurned my Comanche princess because of her taste for these specialties. The best result of my progress in accustoming myself ot the life of the prairie was the weakness I found myself feeling for one of the Cheyennes!

In features, figure, and manner the object of my interest reminded me of my lost, or rather spurned, Comanche. But she did not resemble my princess in dress, for she wore almost no garb at all, as she was the wife of the greatest idler, drunkard, and gambler in the tribe. Her married status did not, however, keep anyone from paying court to her if he felt himself in a position to win her favor in return and to ransom her from her good-for-nothing husband.

Among the Cheyennes there prevailed a strange law with respect to the defense of women against a brutal husband. If a wife found a lover who would pay her husband the price of a divorce, in a sum equal to that which her husband had given her father for the marriage, she was his for the lover to take and wed.

The woman of my choice was attractive. All the charms native to the Indian were present in her person. Though hardly more than a child, she was a hard worker. Her industrious ways attracted and captivated me. I was ready and anxious to settle down and I needed a wife. I decided to buy her from her husband. For a month I took advantage of every opportunity to make my way to her wigwam whenever her husband was gambling at the tribal campfire. I took her gifts, I flattered her, I promised her the pleasantest treatment, a golden future. Finally she yielded to my persuasions and permitted herself to be taken.

I took her to my stockade. The next day her husband appeared, saw her through the spaces between the palisades, and proceeded to complain to the chiefs of the tribe. Forthwith the elders gathered in council. The woman did not want to leave me, and so they let me keep her, after I had paid five ponies and two mules,—the best ponies and the toughest mules. On my part this was a big price, but she was so charming, and so attracted to me, that I'd have sacrificed half my stud rather than give up my good wife. For a week we lived in very paradise.

On the eighth day, when I woke at dawn, I did not find her at my side. My charming wife, my diligent housewife, had vanished, leaving in my courtyard tracks to show which way she had taken. Following those divine footsteps, I pursued her across the prairie until I arrived at—the tepee of her first husband! There I found her quietly occupied in cutting buffalo meat into strips for drying. She was going about her chores in that tepee just as if she had never left it!

I raged, I threatened, I scolded, wept, and tried to get her to tell me why she had left me. Instead of answering, she called her husband. He came and joined her in jeering at me.

I went to the chief. Again the elders met in council. They took up my case and discussed it at length, expressing pity for my position. Then they summoned the pair before a court. I insisted that my wife be returned to me, as I had gone through all the formalities of purchasing her, without any bargaining or haggling over the number of livestock to be given for the deal. The chief confessed that the woman belonged to me and that the husband was not opposed to her return.

"Take your wife," that good-for-nothing said. "She came back to me uninvited. I won't stop her from going back to you. I don't have any desire for her. But I do want your mustangs and mules. Take her or leave her, but I'll never give back those animals. I'll keep the bargain: I'll return the goods, but the pay I'll keep."

So it was up to the woman. And she did not want to go with me. The custom of the Cheyennes, moreover, prevented me from forcing her. Had I bought the girl from her father I could have forced her, but having made the deal with her husband, even the chief could not compel her to accompany me to my dwelling against her will, though her first husband honestly wanted to carry out his part of the agreement.

The girl protested against the decision of the elders, declaring that she preferred a fellow-tribesman to me, and that she didn't want to live in any stockade or stuffy cabin, separated from her own people.

After lengthy discussion, the elders agreed that the woman had the right to choose between rivals. They also handed down the verdict that if she remained with her first husband, he would not be obliged to return the ponies and mules.

So my "treasure" returned to her first husband of her own free will, and it was decided that if my ponies and mules should of *their* free will escape from him and return to my stockade, I was free to keep them.

The loss of my beauty I got over very quickly, but grieved for long over the loss of those fine ponies and those tough mules.

Here Langenor paused and roughed up his hair, as if hesitating out of shame to go on with the rest of his story. After a short interruption, however, he continued.

Those brigands had really out-smarted me. Every step of the deal, as I found out, had been planned in advance. My treasure, by her plot, changed her good-for-nothing beggar of a husband into an Indian of property. She paid the elders their share of the deal, and in cahoots with them made sport of me. Her week-long love for me was all pretense. She had sold herself at the bidding of her worthless husband.

Well, I confess that from then on I managed all kinds of little deals with the redskins in general and the Cheyennes in particular. It was not long before I won back my loss, with a good percentage of profit to boot, proceeding in accordance with the law of the prairie: an eye for an eye, a tooth for a tooth. The Cheyennes soon were convinced that instead of a young greenhorn they had met in me a more accomplished seducer of horses than the professional prairie thieves. Having got back what according to local concepts was recompense for my first loss, and for the time consumed in the trial (capital as well as court costs and expenses), I told myself, "Now you're quits." With that I resumed a regular life, with my old habits.

My success in outwitting them in their little plot riled the Cheyennes, and so they told me that I'd have to leave their territory or lose my scalp. Not wishing any bloody encounters in so futile a cause, I gathered up my movable possessions and betook myself across the River Platte to the newly opened country through which the railroad was being built. Today this is part of the state of Nebraska.

CHAPTER FOUR

Escape from Emma

—Cured of ideals, I made up my mind to go to farming. I would do this among the white farmers on the frontier, of whose naivete, disinteredness, and freedom from Indian trickery I had heard so much. These farmers, I had read in various novels, observed the traditions and customs of Arcadia. They lived idyllically, like the shepherds you read about in Gessner.[30] They were in love only with beauty and virtue. Their daughters gave their favors to the most industrious suitors, and their mothers knew nothing of the art of capturing rich sons-in-law.

Leaving my livestock in the care of ranchers along the North Platte, I wandered along the river. Several hundred miles below the ranch I found a country actually like a bit of Arcadia itself, inhabited by a people pretending to be very naive. So I took up a claim in the river valley, near a grove. I built myself a cabin beside a small spring that gushed forth from beneath blossoming grass. My cabin was a fine one for that part of the country and the conditions there, as it had three rooms. I covered the walls inside with painted paper and with pictures from the weekly newspapers. This kind of decoration is, as you know, considered the height of elegance on the frontier.

I put up shelves, and arranged rows of pots and pans and all the vessels I needed for the produce of my dairy. I drove a series of pegs underneath the shelves, for cloths and clothing. I bought a churn, and two cows, and dug a cellar. I sent to Lincoln for five dollars worth of seed and planted a little garden in front of my windows. Without picking and choosing among the seeds, I sowed them all together, hit or miss, and every single seed I put in the ground came up. No botanist would be able to distinguish in this chaos the pansies from the cabbage, asters from carrots, lillies from onions.

My garden, the only one in the neighborhood, made me famous among the farmers roundabout. A red-haired farmer from across the river, the Croesus of the county, took the first opportunity he could find to come and have a look at my establishment. He praised the illustrations on the walls and the stables, which were constructed not of adobe but boards. He was absolutely charmed as his eyes roved about my fields swaying with young wheat. And he should have been, for I had invested every bit of my capital in land and seed.

I was not in the habit, thanks to my lonely life and the experiences I had been through, of confiding my business interests to strangers, and so I did not tell anyone about the livestock I had left on the North Platte. But even without knowing about this, my neighbors decided that I had a good start for a young pioneer.

From time to time my neighbor from across the river would bring his wife and young daughter to look at my garden and papered walls. Flaxen-haired Emma, her fingers rosier than the dawn (probably from milking the cows every day!), was the farmer's oldest olive-branch, and she was enchanted with the vegetables and the lady-birds, but the illustrations on the walls didn't charm her so much as the hooks I had put up to hang clothes on. "Papa ought to follow your example," she said, "and put up hooks in our house. But papa isn't interested in making women comfortable."

Without going into further discussion of adventures of this nature in that rural Arcadia, I'll just say that all the neighbors, one after the other, maintained that I ought to get married. A farmer without a wife was like a fish without water, they said. What could a fish do without water, or a farmer without a wife? And so, before I could look around, they had entangled me in an engagement with the flaxen-haired, worthy, but devilishly taciturn Emma.

Ach, I could not sit beside her that another, also flaxen-haired, did not appear without being invited! I thought that I had forgotten about her. That lost one out of my past had never presented herself in the days of my two Indian maidens. The lowliness of their position in society permitted of no comparison. But scarcely did that white-cheeked little goose from along the Platte open her blue eyes wide than for the first time I began to whisper coldly some sentimental confessions, when even after the first embrace she reminded me of cows——I felt a kind of nausea, gritted my teeth, and thought of the lost one yonder. I dispelled all poetic promises and did not even attempt to strike fire with this plump country-bumpkin creature, without heart or soul, who could speak of nothing at all except to tell me how to manage my establishment.

I persuaded myself finally that I had to adjust myself to my surroundings. Having decided to settle here, I had to accommodate my style of living to that of the natives. I could not find a better helpmeet than this accomplished and good-looking farm girl. Unfortunately, however, despite the logic of my decision it seemed to me that the mosquitoes flying over us as I led her home in the evening along the river, buzzed with malicious laughter, that the moon grimaced at me and gazed with the eyes of an old sly-boots who had seen so many times the absurdity of youth that it could not consent to my commonsense courting. And when I was back in my lonely cabin, every print on the wall brought back the features of that lost one across the ocean.—

Here I interrupted Langenor.

"I don't want to pry into any secrets you may have, but if you don't mind, tell me,—why did you leave that one? Did she betray you? Did she leave you for someone else? Did her family, or the conditions of her life, prevent the union?"

Langenor hesitated before answering, but finally managed to give me a short confession.

—Well, I was always different from those of my age in boldness at crucial moments in affairs of the heart. A hundred times I scolded myself for such foolishness, and others did the same, but I could never cure myself of the weakness. She—the one we are speaking of—never heard from my lips a single request for her hand. But the two of us were educated under the same roof, since as a very young child I lost my parents and was placed in the care of hers. As a boy I visited her home. I was sure she understood my feelings, that she knew why I struggled even beyond my strength to create a future worthy of her. Did she not give me signs time after time that she felt her power over me? And yet in spite of this she flirted with others, and when my efforts to assure a means of livelihood for myself took a long time to realize, the very next day after I had received word of a position, a thunderbolt fell on my head from a clear sky. I was informed that my adored one had accepted another, whose chief virtue was a high position in society. The old story,—no use repeating it. My further life you might call a series of absurdities, ending with my hiding away in these mountains. But when she did me that wrong I was very young, and desperately in love.

And she?

I don't know what she is doing, where she is making her life. A few hours before leaving Europe, in fact just as I was about to embark, a letter was handed me from a friend. In it I found a hint to the effect that she had taken my disappearance to heart, that it plunged her in tears and upset her family, who feared that she would not shake off the disappointment of this premature sorrow.

This new evidence of her fickleness did not change my plans. I told myself it was too late. Actually what was I to do, throw myself between her and that other suitor? The ship hissed, whistled, bells rang, the foam churned... I went on deck at the last minute. Then land faded from sight and my pain was assuaged.

From the day I arrived in the West I have had no word from her, and no one at home has had one of me. We here do not bother our heads with letters. We don't enrich the postal service. With knives and hoes we write more lasting memoirs than any that could be penned. So many thousands of miles separate us. So many years have passed. And so, may God protect her from all evil!—

Langenor's voice grew more and more indistinct as his story proceeded. He spoke in jerks, with long pauses between, and in his speech as he revealed his emotions there was a hesitancy, and even a kind of foreign accent.

A strange thought struck me. Could it be possible?... If his complexion had not become so weathered, if I had not given up trying to tell the difference between nationalities by the lines of the face...but for all that, perhaps I could have justified a certain suspicion that I had. But could a man, although de-nationalized to the extent that he had forgotten his native speech, if he met a fellow-countryman, refrain, on hearing this one's name, from throwing himself at once on his neck? Would he not weep, as he sat beside me on some mountain height, on some piece of silver ore such as in this country of untapped treasure serves as a footstool, would he not have questioned me at length as to what was going on at home, would he not have drunk in the music of sounds so sweetly caressing to the ear?

I did not know until I met Langenor that there were people who, often out of eccentricity, often from unfair attitudes or shame over something in the past, would deny their origin.

Well, the fact is that I was not mistaken as to Langenor. If I had sized him up correctly, it was up to me to watch out and investigate. It was understandable that he should deny his foreign origin among the rapacious gang he lived with, not wishing to bring down upon his head any unpleasantness from those who had no respect for foreigners. Except for my one single self, no one in Montana suspected that Langenor was not an American.

I was eager to confirm my suspicion, and to ask him whether I was right and from what country he had come to America. But before I could commit that sin against American propriety, Langenor resumed his account of his adventures.

—My marriage to Emma was set for shortly after harvest. Unfortunately, however, or rather fortunately for our happiness, there appeared in the valley of the Platte a guest uninvited and unexpected, but diligent. Clouds of grasshoppers fell upon our farms. Fields already golden with the ripening wheat, green gardens and even the pastures and trees, fell victims to these voracious insects. The country that before the onset of this plague looked like Eden itself, appeared, in their wake, but an empty waste.

On my farm not a blade was left. Even my cows died, for lack of pasture.

I went to Emma, whose father's farm the obscene insects had treated more kindly, and asked to have the marriage postponed. Up to that time I had not mentioned to anyone the livestock I had left on the ranch, keeping these as a surprise, a pleasant bit of news for my wedding day. Now I was intending to speak of these, to tell Emma why I was postponing the wedding. I planned on going for my herd, selling it, and with what I made on them, making up for the losses I had suffered on the farm.

But Emma wanted to hear nothing from me. Without letting me tell my plan, she freed me from my vows. This disaster, coming so close to the wedding, she held to be a harbinger of evil, and a warning that we two should remain just friends. Her parents shared her view. I took leave of them all, happier than if someone had put me on a hundred horses. Three days later I heard that some booby whose fields had completely escaped destruction began calling on that perfidious maiden. I congratulated him on his valuable acquisition, but myself I congratulated even more that this particular piece of luck had passed me by.

That's not the end of the story, for the next spring I had revenge on the pair. A horde of young grasshoppers, descendants of those that had ruined me, marched back and forth and up and on over the valley, sparing no one. Emma's parents and her betrothed wrung their hands when they heard that I had returned from along the North Platte with a handsome, plump, well-fed herd. Besides the herd, I had won fame and money to boot on my journey to the Platte. The government paid me handsomely for my service in an encounter with the Indians. My return astounded all my neighbors, and I was the talk of the region. Paying no attention to them and wishing only to get out of a region full of vermin, I sold my land for practically nothing and betook myself to Montana.

As I was passing through the little town I met Emma in the parlor of the hotel. We stood for a minute alone, without witnesses. She wanted to bid me good-bye. She put out her paw, red and rough as usual, but good and warm. She said she would remember me, and that she had broken off with that other fellow, feeling that she could not love him as a God-fearing wife ought to love a husband. She even touched her apron to her eyes... it wasn't snowy-white, and it smeared her little nose.

I clinked my spurs, bowed, mounted my mustang, cracked my whip and with my livestock hurried merrily away toward cold Montana. I looked for a ravine with a good site for my livestock. Finding just the right place, I built a stockade so closely fashioned that no woman's eye could possibly peek through the palisades. I decided to become a hermit monk, and for company I chose an Indian boy...our little red devil, whom I warned not to do any talking or gossiping. It wasn't hard for the lad to obey, as the Indian is by nature taciturn.

That little monster has poisoned my life. Before a quarter of a year had passed in his remarkable company, I felt the old loneliness and restlessness. I remembered even with a little longing the faithless Emma. I grieved for my Comanche princess, and I would have given a hundred oxen to exchange my boy for the unfaithful Cheyenne. If my regrets make you smile, if you do not understand the hopelessness that I suffer, just close yourself up in this stockade with this red devil for a few months, or for the years I have lived here, and test for yourself how the country tastes where they run after a bonnet as if it were something extraordinary!—

The campfire was dying down, and the giant hands of the clock of nature warned us that it was nearly midnight: the long shadows of the lofty mountain that already reached our encampment. Constellation after constellation scattered its sparkling embroidery over and above the pyramid with the diamond cross on its slope.

Langenor broke off his touching story. And we proceeded to get ready for the night. We threw a couple of logs on the fire and cleared the pebbles from the place where we were going to sleep. With our knives we dug out holes for our hips, and, turning our boots with their high heels upward as protection against the night moisture, we wrapped ourselves tightly in blankets and buffalo hides and in a twinkling were sound asleep.

CHAPTER FIVE

The Over-Eager Modiste

The next two nights we spent in excruciating misery. And even that night at the foot of The Holy Cross a wind sprang up, at first warm and sticky with mist, but colder and colder as morning came on. The wind woke me up, as it brought back in my joints all the rheumatic pains I had ever suffered. Those pains, I might say, are the common lot of all wanderers, who camp and sleep out of doors, in mist and dew, frost and rain.

Langenor slept right on, never waking until rain began pouring down in buckets and roused that iron figure. The dastardly wind crept through the valley, veiled the mountain with leaden clouds, and filled the whole expanse around us with an ominous roar.

The storm lasted unexpectedly long, defying the rules of the Montana climate, which prides itself in summer on its cool and stable weather seldom interrupted except by brief showers.

Now, for two days the slopes of the mountains roared with a thousand cascades the color of brick. Floods of water poured from the branches of every tree. Clouds of mist filled the air, and above these the tops of the trees and the needles glistened with snow, for what fell in the valley as water was turned on the summits to snow. The highest peaks were hidden in clouds of mist, and there was a menacing roar among the fir trees. Rocks, loosened by the rain, came free and rolled down. Branches, broken off by the tempest, blocked our path. Everything seemed threatened with extermination. Our compass showed us which direction we should take, but with conditions as they were, with everything around us in confusion,—streams so swollen that they carried off whole rocks and trees,—we did not dare follow the advice of that instrument. As to animal life, it was all in hiding. And it was impossible, because of the rain, to keep a campfire going. Our teeth chattered from hunger and cold, and we had to pull in our belts a notch or two.

When the worst of the deluge had abated and there was only an occasional shower of hail and snow, we hurried as fast as we could on our way. It was dangerous, wherever we tried to go, as every hill was pouring down its own Niagara, gliding majestically along and sending up clouds of flying snow that looked like steam. Before our eyes, right in the midst of summer, we had scenes of winter before our eyes. Under our feet the soft snow rolled up into little balls.

Sometimes we would find a gentle slope, covered with snow, and this we would slide down, alpine fashion, with the speed of a locomotive. Those interludes were the only pleasant moments in our journey home. Fortunately the wind was at our backs, so that we did not have the banners of snow hitting us directly in the eyes.

Freezing and soaked to the skin, we finally reached Langenor's quiet canyon. The squatter had chosen his valley with such wisdom and foreknowledge that his stockade never knew what it was to experience the fury of an alpine tempest. And so, after days of misery and hunger, we at last met a stag. We shot him and were able to refresh ourselves, get warmed through at a campfire, drink pure water, and rest at night on soft grass, in the midst of fragrant blossoms and in the silence of fir trees not being battered and broken by the wind.

Above us, however, the clouds of mist still rolled. Every peak was snow-covered, and the serried ranks of the mountains looked like alabaster obelisks on granite pedestals. But the ice up there on the summits no longer bothered us. Only two hours journey, and we knocked on the gate of the stockade. The Indian boy opened it for us. Langenor's thought was above all for his cattle. The poor oxen had their tongues hanging out, their sides were sunken in, and they were wheezing. From their woeful looks, Langenor knew the poor things had not been let out to graze from the moment the storm began. Langenor sighed but held his tongue. I suppose he was used to such things from his Indian boy.

The condition of the cabin was even worse than that of Langenor's treasured herd. The boy had consumed all the delicacies held in waiting for special guests, and had opened a demijohn of whiskey and drunk it up, every drop. In a word, he had played every trick only a young rascal could think of when left alone in a bachelor's establishment.

Langenor sighed, beat his arms piously, and groaned, "Oh Lord, grant me a housekeeper, or a padlock!"

That evening, after repairing damages and straightening everything out, Langenor put his feet up on that iron stove of his, cut himself a slab of tobacco big enough to last until midnight, and began scolding himself for the last lost opportunity he had had, when pure luck, of its own accord, dropped in his hands. If only he had grasped the opportunity, instead of that little red devil waiting for him in his cabin, he would have had a very angel in the flesh! Or so it seemed now.

"Imagine," he said. "It wasn't more than a year ago when this poor cabin was host to a miraculous apparition. She came, filled my cabin with light, smiles, the fragrance of the best perfumes you can buy in Helena, and the rustle of gowns of beautiful material..."

Here Langenor paused to muse and beat his forehead.

"Then she vanished, leaving darkness, disorder, the silence of the grave, longing..."

"How did it happen, and who was this apparition?" I asked.

With this Langenor told the following story.

—For several months I hadn't paid a visit to either Helena or Virginia City, and since I had had no guests here, it had been a long time since I'd heard a human voice. I'd warned that devil of an Indian long before never to start talking to me, not even a single word, and this was all to the good with him, as Indians prefer snoring and chewing to conversation.

After a long period of complete silence, one day there came to my ears the pleasant sound of hoofbeats. I hurried out of my stockade.

Imagine what I saw! In front of my gate, a young and charming lady. She was riding a small Indian pony and leading another horse, fully saddled.

The apparition dazzled me. I lost my tongue and couldn't even recognize her for a second, though actually I knew who she was. I had often heard of her and even seen her in Helena. She had invited me to her home, but with my customary unreasonableness, I had not gone.

There were various whispers circulated about her, but only whispers, thanks to the respect even the wildest pioneers have for womankind. Furthermore, all the whisperings had to do with her past, somewhere far away in the east, or even in Europe. All that was ancient, unimportant history.

If we were to examine the past of every gentleman and lady who arrives here, there would be no living in Montana. What difference does it make if this one or that one played some trick a thousand miles from here, ten years ago, and managed to escape the police, if he conducts himself with propriety among us? Nor should it be any concern of ours if the lady who conducted the only women's clothing store in Helena escaped from the eyes of some stepmother or guardian and by herself found her way here among people who, while coarse and crude, were not dangerous to anyone but males.

The lady's business was going very well. More than one rich miner respected her very footsteps. But she picked and chose among her admirers and held them all at bay. Perhaps this was in fact the reason for those whispers. She alone, of all the women I knew in Helena, dressed as the climate dictated, and with taste. She was sure of herself, aware of all the good points of her face, figure, and mind, and knew how to show these off in the best light. When other women tried to erase the marks of their sex, to assume the coarse manners of their surroundings, she remained a woman in the full sense of the word. Sensible, a kind of Junoesque type, not too young, she belonged to that order of women who made the journey, however imprudently, to California, Nevada and other mining areas in the wake of the gold fever.

I doubt, however, whether any of the lady's sisters of the road understood as well as she how to profit from the material conditions existing here without being severely criticized. The thought never entered my head that I who had been spurned by the daughter of a poor farmer might aspire to the hand of the most beautiful person in Helena. Her reckless visit to me in my cabin was in contrast to her well-known tact, and for this reason struck me with the force of a bolt of lightning from a clear sky.

"Hello, there," called my Amazon visitor, with an expression of pretended anger. "Has constant preoccupation with gloomy nature made Langenor forget how to greet a guest,—especially a lady?"

She was right in scolding me as, instead of helping her alight from her saddle, I just stood there gaping at her. But she did have very beautiful eyes, and her black tresses hung low in her neck and were tossed about by the free wind...

I led her to the stockade, helped her dismount and with my own hand unsaddled her horses and led them to the stable, seeing to it that my small Indian gave them corn. When I finally went to my cabin, I found my guest had taken possession of the place and made herself right at home. She had discarded her riding habit, washed her face and hands, straightened the hang of the cracked mirror, and started looking around in the pantry, saying that her journey had given her an unusual appetite.

I began setting the table, with her helping me, seeming to know by instinct where the plates and spoons were kept. I was going to cook something, but she drove me out of the kitchen, laughing good-naturedly, and rolled up her sleeves so that charming little dimples were revealed in her white arms,—a sight fatal to the hermit. Her little fingers probed among the cooking utensils until I was jealous of them myself, and of that velvet touch. I thought of the hundreds of days when I had gone about that work with my ungainly ways.

When she had finished what she was about in the kitchen, she summoned me to dinner...sat down beside me, letting the folds of her dress drape themselves about me. I began thinking of Emma, my Indian wife of two weeks, and the Comanche maiden in New Mexico. My guest told me she had been visiting my nearest neighbor, a married man, who owed her for goods purchased by his wife. He couldn't pay her in money, but gave her a skin, which would do for one payment.

The bold creditor was returning home following the successful outcome of this business deal. She boasted of the way she had handled it and declared that in a thousand women you wouldn't find one who could manage it as well as she.

Her words had an effect on me exactly opposite to what I expected, as I began at once to look with terror into the soul of this Amazon who was able to outwit trappers in a business deal and stop for a rest in the cabin of a bachelor. Not noticing my silence, she chattered on about her success in Helena and of how she had done it all without help. People take advantage of her lonely state, she said, and are slow to pay. She was surprised that I wasn't bored to death in this silent ravine. She pitied me, living all alone, neglected, in disorder... And all the while I was such a dunce that I did not comprehend the drift of these allusions, though to anyone else they'd have been crystal clear!

She inquired whether there were trout in my little stream, and deer in the forest. She remarked on how pleasant it would be to have for one's own such a pleasant corner, to spend a few days there in the summer, hunting, tramping in the mountains, listening to the splashing of the cascade. And to have as a companion in all this one whose heart responds to every charm of nature, every manifestation of noble feelings on the part of man.

I was tempted for a moment to offer her the hospitality of my cabin, to invite her for a week of fishing, hunting, listening to the murmur of the mountain torrents.—

"And did you offer yourself along with all this?" I interrupted.

"No. I could not insult her. If she had accepted my offer, what would you have called her? What would the neighbors have said, what would all Helena have said?"

"You thick-head! She was trying to make you understand that she liked you. She was throwing down her glove, challenging you, trying to transplant you to Helena, among her acquaintances there. Telling you she wanted you to leave these miserable surroundings, go to Helena and live the way God meant a man to live, with a wife more capable than you could find anywhere in the country."

— To tell you the truth, although I did not understand at first the drift of her conversation, I began to when she spoke of matters of the heart. But right at that moment a third figure joined us at the table. Between myself and her sat this third figure: a phantom from the past. I saw this being clearly... I could not begin... I compared this modest, home-grown violet with the full-blown, reckless rose of the West, and I couldn't say a word. My silence angered my guest. She got up from the table and summoned the Indian boy, ordered him to saddle her horse, as it was already two o'clock in the afternoon and she had a six-hour journey ahead of her, which would make it difficult for her to reach home before dark, even on this July day.

The boy hurried to carry out her command. She, meanwhile, ranged about the cabin, fanning herself energetically. Only once did I break the silence, to ask her how she liked Montana and the companionship of men almost exclusively or of women who have become like men.

"Oh my God," she replied, impatiently, "who is there in this world, anyway, that gets all he wants in life? I came here seeking forgetfulness, and in the years I've been here I've been lucky enough to get more than that, as I've done very well for myself. And so I've grown fond of the country, though at first it gave me only hell. I'm sorry to leave it. I'd like to stay here forever, but unfortunately, it seems that higher considerations do not permit that. I must think of the future and change the course of my life, which at present is not suitable for a woman."

"How's that? You're thinking of leaving?"

"I can't foresee the future... if it turns out that I leave these mountains, I'll say farewell with a heartfelt tear. Even in Helena I've met a number of noble souls, from whom I shall part not without regret."

I may be mistaken, but it seemed to me that I could detect a despairing, suppressed moan in her voice, and that I could see a tear glistening in her wide, burning eyes, which at that moment were turned on me almost beseechingly. But before I could make sense out of my feelings, the boy called from the courtyard that the horses were ready. She hesitated the slightest second, gave me her hand, which I took lightly, coldly. Her eyes shone with fire, her face burned, paled... She bit her lips and ran from the cabin, not waiting for me to help her, and mounted her horse with the boy's help. Once again she turned toward me, as if she regretted her ecstasy of the minute before.

"And when shall we be seeing you in Helena?" she asked, in the low voice of a siren.

"The usual time, when the cattle have finished grazing."

I couldn't possibly describe the scornful expression of her eyes as for a moment they measured me from top to toe as if I were some monster.

"Ha! Ha! Ha!" she snorted with a smile that no one could deny was forced. "Ha! Ha! Ha! Mr. Langenor has dedicated himself completely to the bucolic life. He's concentrated all his thoughts in the shambles of Helena! And so, adieu. And it is adieu...farewell...for it is probable I shall be leaving before autumn when you come to town."

Furious, she gave the spur to her horse. Before I could gather my thoughts, the hoofs of the mustangs were already wakening echoes in the canyon, and the rocks along her path clanked beneath the feet of her galloping steeds.

I stood for a moment, stupefied. Then I went back to my cabin and began figuring out what it was that had made the woman so angry, why she had gone off in such a fury. Suddenly the light shone in my head as in seven churches.

"Away with that phantom!" I shouted. "Away with the gloomy memories of the past. Grasp the gold of reality! Boy, saddle a mustang for me, and be quick about it!"

Not waiting for the boy to do as I'd bid, I went myself to the stable, threw a Mexican saddle on the first horse that came to hand, and not finding a bridle in the straw, grabbed a lasso to serve as a bridle, and tore off after the Amazon at breakneck speed.—

"Did you catch up to her?"

Langenor gave me a look of utter scorn, surprised that I should ask him such a question.

"If I had caught up with her, do you think I'd be living here alone, morose as a badger? In my haste, I did not notice which horse I was taking. My mustang started to limp. He stumbled, and I couldn't get him up with the poor bridle. He fell, and bruised me so that I was hardly able to get myself back to the stockade. A week passed before I could so much as sit on a horse. As soon as I had my powers back, I made straight for Helena."

"And she had gone, I suppose? Woman don't put up with the kind of brush-off you gave her."

"Yes, she'd gone. To Utah, they said. She had received threats. Even her house and shop bore the mark of some French adventuress."

"Why such haste?"

"Wait a moment. That night I did not sleep in Helena, but in an express train. You know that our postal service is undependable. To Utah was a journey of no more than a few days. I'd hardly shaken off the dust of travel and found myself a hotel, when I began looking for my lost one. I was told that a foreign lady had arrived not long ago at the fort which rises above the Mormon city of Salt Lake. Uncle Sam's garrison maintains watch from there over the refractory followers of Brigham Young.

"The modiste from Helena lived there, as I found out, it is true, but as the wife of one of the officers. A certain lieutenant, on leave in Helena, met her and proposed marriage, and received an equivocal answer. For a few days she vanished from his sight, and then, on returning, she accepted his hand. Telling no one in Helena of their plans, the two suddenly departed. No one in Helena had any idea of what caused the beautiful modiste to leave the town."

"And did you meet her after that?"

"Before I left Utah I met her, but in the company of others. I was obliged while I was in the city to spend a good deal of time in various groups of people. You probably know that people around these parts take me for some kind of hero, a chief of some sort, and invite me around. I do not deserve the reputation that I have. The small service I was able to perform has been blown up to make me a model of unimaginable virility and intelligence."

Langenor hurried over the last sentence. The innate modesty of the misanthrope did not permit him to make it clear just why the people of the region regarded him as a hero. But wherever I went before meeting him I was told of the reasons for his fame. I was eager to hear more, and so interrupted the course of his story to make him tell me exactly what he had done.

CHAPTER SIX

The Hero of Plum Creek

—If you wanted to find out why I have such an exaggerated reputation, you'd have to listen all night long to various adventures I've had among the Indians. But my principal service was the one on the River Platte, when I saved an emigrant train, made up for the most part women and children, from an attack by Cheyennes.

The attack took place on the route of the great railroad to the Pacific. A long series of wagons, filled with unarmed people, halted beside a cabin that passed for a railway station, at the mouth of Plum Creek,[31] where the stream enters the Platte. A deluge had destroyed the bridges beyond this station and interrupted the movement of the railroad, holding it up for a week.

At this time all the Indian tribes were to the south of the railroad, waiting in order, by a final despairing attack to cut the streak of iron rails, whose existence threatened them with defeat and capture by the white man. War to the death, the last in the history of the West in which the Indians had a chance of winning, raged on the prairie. Not a week went by without some effectual attack or a train derailment, and horrible massacre. The officials in Plum Creek, fearing for the fate of the emigrants if they remained near the station, sent help, but the nearest division of the army was so far away that it couldn't reach the place for several days.

Just at this time I was leading my cattle in that direction from along the North Platte. I had several Pawnees helping me. Pawnees, as you know, were always faithful allies of the white man, and the prairie knows no braver and no more knightly tribe of redskins than these. Their loyalty to us won them the hatred of all their brother Indians. Every Indian hand is against them, and we have taken care of them so badly that the Sioux have in fact almost wiped out the whole tribe.

In Plum Creek I found frightful confusion. A spy had brought word that bands of Cheyennes were gathering not very far away. If these knew of the unarmed condition of the station and the amount of booty to be had there, to say nothing of the number of victims, they would certainly fall upon the place like a flock of vultures. You can imagine the fate awaiting those travelers, those women, those children.

I wrung my hands in despair at the thought of this and cursed my own ineptitude, that I couldn't save all those innocent people.

One of the Pawnees showed me a way to do something. His sharp glances over the prairies during our journey had detected traces of brother Pawnees. He said that a division of the tribe was hunting on a high prairie across the river. To find these huntsmen would not be easy, since probably they were always on the move, camping first in one place, then in another. I decided, anyway, to seek them out, with my Pawnee informer as guide.

How difficult our search was, you may know from the fact that for a full twenty-four hours I never dismounted from my horse.

On cruelly tired mustangs we were making for a defended postal station on the route from Plum Creek to Denver. A stockade showed up in the distance, but I did not leave the route we were following in order to tell the garrison what was going on, or to ask for a fresh horse. They did not know me, and might refuse to help me, and I had no money with me.

Several horses belonging to the station were grazing at a distance from the place. I took two of the best, and hurried on my way. If the people at the station had got hold of me, who knows if they would not have pronounced judgment on me and have hanged me on the spot, without listening even to an explanation. In those days and place horse-stealing was a capital crime.

The horses did not serve us very long. A horde of unfriendly Indians met us on the open prairie far from help. In accordance with the custom of the prairie, we dismounted and shot our horses, then used their bodies as a fortification from behind which to shoot at the enemy. For three hours we defended ourselves against twenty of those redskins.

Indians are most afraid of a white man when he has something to protect him from their arrows and something on which to support his gun. And so, despite their greater numbers, they did not dare fall upon our defense directly, but withdrew a little way and shot at us from a distance. This method of warfare was in our favor as long as we had enough ammunition, and during the daylight hours. But night was coming on, and it looked as if night would see the earth running with our blood.

I looked toward the west. The sun was already reddening the tall grass. Never had it seemed to me so marvelous.

Two charges were all we had left,—not for the enemy, but for ourselves. The frontiersman who knows what a horrible fate, what miseries, await the prisoner of an Indian tribe will never let himself be taken. Our attackers, unaware as yet of our lack of ammunition, and having themselves lost several of their company, while waiting in the darkness and letting their horses graze, kept their eyes fixed on us. Sometimes when one of us would raise his head above the barricade of the bodies of our horses, they would shoot at us. It was those shots that saved us. In the silence of the night they could be heard a considerable distance away. Before the night was over, the prairie was covered with dust from beneath the hoofs of a new Indian band.

The newcomers frightened our attackers away. They vanished in the twinkling of an eye, like some fata morgana of the steppe. The newcomers drew near, and soon my guide was able to recognize his fellow-tribesmen. Those very Pawnees whom we had been looking for so long, hearing our shots, took account of them and began looking for us. They set us free, and at my request betook themselves toward Plum Creek. Thus I had with me fifty of the most valorous Bedouins of the West.

We passed a herd of buffaloes, who shook their heads in wonder that horsemen did not shoot them down. This had gone on until the greed of humankind had slaughtered a million herds of these meek giants and made them as rare as the European bison. The high plain above the bed of the Platte was reddened from moving columns of these cattle. There were so many of them massed together that they delayed our progress, but we managed to get to Plum Creek ahead of the Cheyennes, who were reported to be advancing in great strength toward certain victory.

Not stopping to inquire whether military forces or railroad officials were to be found at the station, I took charge there. I put a revolver to the temple of the first official who protested and ordered the Pawnees to tie him up. As a reward for the Pawnees' help, I collected money from the travelers and divided it among the Indians.

Then I ordered the small building which served as a station and as a hotel for the emigrants barricaded. I put the travelers inside this. In the railroad train I found no weapons, but did discover a package of uniforms and military caps that were on their way from Washington to the garrison in Utah. These gave me a wonderful idea. I ordered the uniforms taken out and divided among the Pawnees. Time was pressing...in a couple of hours after my return there shone on the other side of the river the feathers adorning the heads of the Cheyennes.

As they crossed Plum Creek and began making their way to the ford on the Platte, I was able to count them. Half a tribe were making this foray. And to show that they were certain of victory, they had brought with them their mules and squaws, so that they could pack up the booty. There must have been a hundred and fifty armed Indians surrounding us.

I ordered several Pawnees to cross the ford and start shooting, so as to hold back our enemies until I could finish my preparations. The patrol fulfilled my command in splendid fashion. Shooting from behind bushes on the riverbank, the Pawnees held the Cheyennes back for several minutes. When finally they had to give up, as the whole horde came down upon them, my principal division was ready for the fight. Meanwhile, my Pawnees had removed their feathers and Indian accoutrements and every one of them had put on the deceptive uniform but without putting their arms in the sleeves and fastening only the top button, so that they could more easily throw off the garb. On each head there now sat a field-cap! I led the attack, trying to keep them in line as far as I could, a thing that was not easy, as when Indians go into battle they scatter, and do not know how to hold a line.

The Cheyennes were stunned at sight of an army. In order to match half a squadron of regular cavalry they had to be in full strength. And so they did not cross the river, but held back and withdrew to the other side of the stream.

But in me and my Pawnees the blood was already boiling. We smelled victory without counting the enemy. In our fashion as westerners, we crossed the river at the ford and went after them on a trot. They had taken up an excellent position and though they did not feel strong enough to attack, did not hesitate to fight a defensive engagement.

They stood some several hundred steps beyond the small bridge over the stream, at the only crossing point where Plum Creek flows in a channel with perpendicular banks. Their idea was to let us cross the bridge so that then they could fall upon us with their Indian warwhoops, and frighten our horses. Redskins count strongly on those warwhoops in their encounters with the regular cavalry. Their hellish cries scare the wits out of the army horses, which are not accustomed to such a reception.

Because of this type of warfare, the Cheyennes, who did not dare attack a small band of Europeans standing in one place, shooting with long-range arms, profited greatly when Europeans attacked offensively. With regular cavalry I would never have dared cross that bridge and, leaving a frightful abyss beside us, expose the army to the Indians' uproar.

But the situation was different here. The bridge resounded beneath the hoofs of our horses. The hearts of the Cheyennes must have beat high with joy at sight of Uncle Sam's cavalry advancing right into their trap. When I had crossed the bridge and as I began to round up my column, they leapt from the hill like twisting devils. Already they were but fifteen steps from us. Then, just at that moment, the Pawnees threw off their uniforms and caps. Naked, their bronze skins glistened in the morning sun. Warwhoop answered warwhoop, the beat of their gallop replied to that of our horses.

Our horses did not take fright, but their mustangs did. They tried to hold them in check, but in vain. The frightened Indian pony does not know the meaning of spur or restraining hand. Every Cheyenne mustang turned around and could not be held back. Some fell and escaped. We trampled them down and pursued them with strength tripled by our success thus far. We caused a horrible massacre, without losing on our side a single horse or man.

And so there you have the reason for my reputation, and the source of the dollars I told you I have in the bank. Out here they pay you for such deeds.

As to how the word of it got around, in Utah there lived more than one witness of that encounter on Plum Creek, since among the travelers on that occasion were to be found families of the men who had settled in the Mormon capital. And so I was lavishly received in all the most distinguished homes, when I went to Salt Lake in search of my lost one.

Finally they even arranged a fete in my honor one evening, so that all could gaze upon the hermit who understood Indian methods of warfare. The guests gathered in a villa just outside the city. There was a garden, with lights and artificial fires.

Nothing is so amusing, my dear fellow, as celebrations by the petit bourgeois! The poor things ruin themselves, and the result of their efforts turns out to be more amusing than the mouse that the mountains in labor produce. Trees were hung with many colored Chinese lanterns... The moon rose from above the mountains, so that with its marvelous glitter it dimmed the light of the candles in the lanterns, revealing the undependable nature of the illumination. The entire fete was a failure. We were bitten unmercifully by mosquitoes and the ladies fled from the garden, complaining of the insects and also of the dew, as no paths had been cleared. The parlor inside the villa couldn't accommodate the guests. In a word, I was embarrassed for my hosts.

But it was on this occasion that I saw my lost one and her husband. Just a single glance she gave me, to tell me she remembered, and then turned quickly away. Her husband greeted me with open, soldierly manner. I was told that besides his military rank, he also had other means. Obviously he adored her, and so she must have counted herself fortunate. I had no desire to poison her good fortune, or to tear her away from the one she was bound to forever. But after supper, while the men were at the table drinking my health and the ladies had left their company, I went outdoors for a moment to cool my burning head.

It was then I met her, on the veranda, in the dusk. Did she know I would not remain in the salon flowing with wine,... that I would be sure to go out? Was she waiting for me deliberately? I do not know, but the fact is, she was standing there, all in white, her face bathed in the white light of the moon...whiter than her gown.

"And so I meet you once more!" I said in a low voice.

"Hush," she whispered. "I am grateful to you for realizing that bygones must be bygones, for not putting in an appearance at the garrison, for playing the role here of a stranger. Everyone whose past life has been full of adventures, failures and successes, conceals something in the secret corners of his memory that he would not wish to display before the eyes of the crowd, something he would like to remain in his heart. I hope to heaven you will forget my first meeting with you, my life in Helena, my visit to you, everything...everything!"

"But tell me," I could not help but say, "tell me why did you visit me that time. As far as I remember, I had met you only once before, and that only casually. You might even have regretted meeting me, since I behaved discourteously, not accepting your invitation. Vanity is not one of my faults. I don't believe you are one to intrude on a stranger, and yet you did, exposing yourself to danger. It would probably be hard to explain the impulse that led you to do this. That excursion of yours was something rash, at least."

"Do you remember that terrible day on the Platte...at the station...how you saved all those victims from death, or from a fate even worse than death? Among those people you saved was a young girl, all alone, orphaned, escaping from a man who from being a guardian had turned into a tyrant. That girl was going she knew not where, anywhere, seeking sanctuary, and trusting to Providence. You did not even give her a glance. You were mad with the fever of battle, proud of your success, and you never noticed in the slightest that young girl, unknown to anyone there, who followed every move of the western hero. That chieftain of the prairie, having repulsed an attack of savage Indians, became the very ideal of that romantic young girl, and in her memory she cherished the picture of her faithful savior as clearly etched as if it had been done by the brush of a master, or by a photographer. Years later, when fate had smiled on that girl, for the second time she was vouchsafed to meet the original of that picture, which still was bright, despite the years. Lonely, exposed to human evil, admonished by common sense that she accept noble care, beaten on by memories, passion, she forgot for a moment all womanly timidity, all feminine shame, and exposed herself to ridicule, to suspicion. Well, in that Montana of yours, much, very much, goes on, and he was so noble that he never betrayed her. And so she saw him once more...and convinced herself that her memory had left not the slightest trace even in his heart. Does that explain it enough for you?"

"Completely. And so...good-bye, madam!"

She gave me her hand. In the salon the lights were brought in. A long, slanting beam shot from the window and lighted on her downcast face. We looked long at each other in that glaring, purple light. Then she turned away from me, slowly... took her hand from mine, and lazily, step by step, slid along the veranda. Then each of us proceeded along his own road.

CHAPTER SEVEN

Boarding House Elite

Following these confidences, I stayed one day more at Langenor's establishment. A quarter of an hour before I was to leave he told me that now he would be lonelier than ever in his silent ravine. I was the very first one, he said, to whom he had revealed all these experiences from his past, the first one from the time of his arrival in the New World who had been able to awaken in him livelier feelings than the intimacy arising from a brief moment in a company with common business interests. And how he would long for me!

"When I think," he said, "that with the exception of that little red devil I won't see a single intelligent face until very autumn, and even then I'll be thrown more often with a wild mob than with people of education, the truth is, I confess, that I wish death would free me right away from such a life."

"Who forces you to such a life? Come back to civilization."

"It's too late! You won't believe how much courage I have to muster to live among people. Even on that visit to Utah, and there you don't find the tone of a capital, I felt an object of ridicule."

"It is only in the eyes of half-barbarians that you would be found laughable. If you mingled with the genuine elements of the better world your shying away from society would not be held against you. And as you familiarized yourself with that world, you would gain self-assurance and soon free yourself of your present fears. You'd remember the customs of youth."

But Langenor did not agree with me nor follow my advice. That strange shyness of his character, which so many times had been the cause of his misery, now bound him to the wild life that he actually had come to hate. He did not wish to return to civilization, nor live again among people whose behavior would remind him, after all, that he could always live in company worthy of himself, that he had wasted all those years for a puff of youthful hopelessness and caprice. Perhaps he was now ashamed of that step, but stubbornly it still remained with him.

This feature of his character confirmed my conviction that Langenor was a Slav. My branch more than all others can not distinguish stubborness and obstinacy from strength of will. The Anglo-Saxon will admit a mistake openly, at the same time sticking tenaciously to what he feels is right. We stick to a mistake with our eyes open, knowing that we are doing wrong but ashamed to confess that, not knowing in the beginning what we were about, we took the wrong road. We stick to ideas whose illogicality we are fully aware of, comforting ourselves obstinately with idle fancies whose absurdity we sometimes feel, deceiving ourselves with the fiction that we are displaying strength of will, when actually we are behaving not as heroes but as stubborn children.

Stubborn Langenor stuck to his fantasies, and so lived in boredom and longing, ashamed to escape from himself and to return to those he belonged with. Perhaps I could persuade him to pull himself out of his misery. Knowing that I could never persuade him to return to the world, I suggested another cure for the woes of loneliness.

"If I were you, I'd never be bored here! You see so many interesting things all around you. Write, why don't you?',

He frowned and answered, "I wouldn't think of spoiling the profit of those scribblers who, finding no themes in their own environment, escape from it into the wilderness."

"Well, teach yourself... These mountains around you, these ravines, these rocks were witnesses to great happenings in bygone years. They are the history of the past recorded for man to read. No Rameses ever carved his deeds on the walls of the pyramids more clearly than did nature here, inscribing its revolutions above us on the snow-covered obelisks up there, and below us on the walls of the canyons. You could gather treasures of knowledge for geologists, study meteorological phenomena, and in this way serve humanity, besides winning for yourself fame of another kind and far more lasting that the reputation of being a good fighter and a perfect shot!

Langenor did not answer. I had no idea whether my advice had struck home or not. But as I mounted my horse, he asked me to get him some books on natural science so that he would have them when he returned to Helena in the fall. I promised I would do so, gave him my hand, and received in response a grasp from fingers that were actually trembling.

We separated for a quarter of a year.

The American autumn, warm, misty, pleasant, had painted the mountains with bright red and gold, and scattered on the withered grass pearls of frost and the brilliance of golden leaves.

How merry were the people of Helena at this time of year! The miners were through for the season on the upper ranges above the city, for winter was already king there, though autumn had still not left the valleys. The miners were gathering for their winter rest in town, bringing with them the booty of a whole summer's labor. Winter was for them a time of waiting, and for the merchants of Helena a season of harvest, from the trade of diggers and squatters, who had left their canyons early, before some unexpected storm filled the trails and tracks, covering the cabins and stockades with twenty-foot deep snow.

I too quartered myself in Helena for the winter, in the cabin belonging to Langenor. He spent most of the winter in this cabin, with the exception of a week, when he put on his snowshoes and despite the cold ranged through the mountains with his traps, changing from squatter to trapper for the time being. It was the custom in these parts for people to have those two careers.

The cabin consisted of a kitchen and bedroom. I left it open and unlocked, according to the custom of the country. No one was afraid of losing his rough furniture or his iron stove, and so no lock was needed. With the exception of rattlesnakes, which greeted me with a hiss when I opened the door the first time, no one had lived in the cabin all summer. I quickly cleaned out these uninvited guests, bought some glass and putty, put in some windows that had been broken by hail, restored the stovepipe, cleaned up the cabin, ordered a few carts of wood and left the logs outside the door. Having got everything in order, I lay down on a bunk above Langenor's bed, and, taking some of his books, waited for my host to arrive.

He arrived with his ponies, dogs, cattle and that devilish little redskin, who had completely forgotten how to speak, as he didn't even grunt out an "umph" now, nor the Indian greeting "how do," when he saw his old acquaintance. Langenor was delighted to find that I had kept my word, and began telling me the monotonous history of his summer occupations. He told me he had sold his cattle to a dealer who would soon be taking them to Fort Benton, not far from the Great Falls of the Missouri. The American government considers that fort as the key to the Great Reservation, the Indian country occupied by the warlike Crows, Blackfeet, etc. And so it maintains in the fort a division of the army. Langenor's cattle would serve the garrison as food all winter long.

Evidence that I had not forgotten my promise comforted Langenor, in the form of the books I had got him, though obviously he could not make full use of them so long as he had to care for his cattle. This would be about ten days, as the dealer wasn't ready yet for the journey down the Missouri.

Every morning Langenor had to go out onto the prairie beyond the city to look after his cattle, who were grazing there on the dry grass of the plain. The pasturage there possessed the virtue common to the grasses of the Far West, in that the first frost, however slight, changes its juicy blades into natural, nutritious and tasty hay. Cattle eat this hay greedily, even though it is buried beneath the snow, and grow fat on it. The cattle were quiet, Langenor fastened his horses on a long lasso and watched over his property, riding his mustang several times a day in order to keep his flock within a narrow circle, all together.

As for myself, during this time I made friends in the town. In a nest so constricted it is easy to get to know everyone you meet. Sound judgment bids you limit your circle of acquaintances, intimacies formed in a place such as this often ending in quarrels, as the cemetery in Helena could readily testify, and tell some interesting stories, too. The oldest inn-keeper of this mordacious settlement could not cite more expressive evidence of the healthy climate of Helena, or of the profit people settling there enjoy so far as hygienic considerations are concerned, than is to be found in the cemetery just mentioned.

"Well sir," he said, "there isn't a soul lying there who died a natural death. People don't get sick in Helena. They don't die of typhus, tuberculosis, dropsy, catarrh of the stomach, or any other diseases. I know every grave there, I assisted at every burial, I have helped to bury forty-six gentlemen, and place the stones on forty-six graves. In the six years of Helena's existence we have buried only forty-six people and every one of them lies there in his boots, with his bowie knife at his belt, as he went about in life and as he died fighting. Yes, sir, that's the way it is."

Not having any desire to be the forty-seventh member of that assortment of valorous and deceased gentlemen, I escaped from that inn and from the miners there. Thanks to my friendship with the local chemist, the sole dandy in the town, who went about in stove-pipe hat and wore stand-up paper collars and a coat of eastern cut, I was received by a certain widow and invited to join a private "chosen circle" of boarders.

The chemist, who was called a metallurgist, since his occupation was principally the analyzing of copper, was at the same time the local veterinary and pharmacist. The telegraph operator, the pharmacist, and several other gentlemen of various "learned" professions, comprised the elite. The circle was presided over by the metallurgist, who was regarded by common consent as the luminary and principal adornment of Helena, as a man of deep learning and Herculean fist.

He was a pedantic Scotsman, with his pockets always crammed with bits of copper and pebbles, his head occupied with the cares of his professions. He larded the converstation always with stories of his scientific triumphs. Everything that happened for good in the region, he attributed to his good counsel. In a word, he had the disgusting habit of always talking about his own prowess and interests.

In our circle of the elite we had women... Daughters of the widow who was our hostess, youthful products of this parochial society, forever strumming their guitars and already casting their sharp glances at the ruddy telegraph operator and balding pharmacist. They had taken a several months' course in the *pension* of a town as fine as Mankato in Minnesota, which numbered more than five thousand inhabitants. There lived there a very old married aunt. Not knowing that I was acquainted with that small western Paris, they described it as the eighth wonder of the world...and for them it was indeed a wonder, with its dozens of "actually plastered" stone dwellings and churches built of stone.

Beneath the amusing surface of this family were hidden positive virtues. How often do you find gold beneath a layer of common clay! The head of the family, a pale, thin widow, bore on her face, which was wrinkled beyond her years, the mark of a lifetime of suffering. Her once delicate hands were rough from the coarse work she was obliged to perform, from the needle and from fire. But from her thoughtful brow and sympathetic eyes, hard work, even hard physical work, had not been able to remove the lines of womanly sweetness, of sympathy for all who suffer, and of faith and the ability to endure. She always reminded me that favoring providence did not leave even the cruel West devoid of those pearls of greatest price,—saintly women. She filled the atmosphere with confidence, hearts were drawn to her, and her sweetness permeated her surroundings. Her life was a series of silent heroisms, not attracting the attention of gawkers, but great, nevertheless, like the deeds of the Maid of Saragossa![32] Unfortunately there was no Byron to sing of these humble and prosaic heroines of the hearth fire.

Having married a good-for-nothing, separated from her kin and from even modest comfort, taken from amongst her family, who loved her, at a very young age, by a harebrained fellow, imprisoned in this terrible Montana cage, having given up hope of a better life, of any change on the fellow's part, or response from him, she did not forsake the betrothed of her youth, nor cast aside that red brass that she had thoughtlessly taken for pure ore. Finally, when at last he reposed outside the town, in the fortieth grave, when she was free to be herself, she demonstrated that the whole of her inheritance as a widow was wrapped up in his children, his name, and his debts. And so that woman who had never in her life read romantic novels or poetry, but shared the principles called by those wiser than herself "feminine Don Quixotism," remained in this wild town with a family of young ladies, with no one to look after her, wearing herself out with back-breaking work, and enduring the caprices of these brutes whom this God-forsaken town took for aristocrats. She stood here, inflexible, in the hope of ransoming belatedly, through the suffering of a proud heart, what she could of the betrothed of her youthful years,—a fellow bankrupt in everything save the love of one woman. And her dedication was understood even by the barbarians of Montana. The wild mob watched over this martyr to principle and love with its rough but genuine care. And she felt the strength of that care, for when her daughters went into town, she could be confident of their return. When after a whole day's work she sat down in front of her fireplace, when she counted the money received from her labor, resting in the fire's orange glare, her lips whispered thankfulness that so many days of bondage had turned out happily, that she had been able to repay so much and that so little remained to pay, that in a year, perhaps two, she would be able to see her daughters holding their heads high among respectable people.

Now and then a wrinkle of sadness would be seen on her face, called there by the sharp word of some guest, or the parochialness of the girls. But this did not happen often, as the girls took from their mother that divine spark of tact which sometimes replaces the schooling of the salon.

Their parochialness did not upset me, even. It is true I never let myself forget that I was in Helena. Perhaps also I excused them freely on account of the goodness of their mother and their own genuine charms, which were a little too full-blown, like the mountains of their homeland. Sometimes I feared that from the bosom of one of these plump maidens a button that was too strained might shoot, and with its whistle might hit me. But despite too full contures and the sturdiness of their motions, one's eye rested gladly on the three graces of Helena, in their clouds of thick golden curls.

The aunt of these three, a younger sister of their mother, who had lived with them for some time, was also a personality in her own right. She was charmed by Helena, Montana, by the metallurgist, by the pharmacist, and in fact even by Langenor, whom she saw every morning through the window. Arriving in Montana for the marriage market in the spring of her twenty-fifth year, she worked hard to remain there, despite her sister's efforts to have her go somewhere else. I have no doubt that this aunt had in her possession a register of every single "catch" in Helena, adding to it a new name every time one of the miners made a good haul or unearthed a rich mine.

The youngest of the three maidens once came to me distracted and told me, incautiously, that her aunt had spurned a half dozen bachelors already, though she had been in Helena only a half year. In the whole town several dozen women were to be found, but bachelors with money could be counted in hundreds, especially in the winter. But the girls' aunt was probably looking for a husband who not only had money, but a stable character! For this the sister had that club of ours of "the elite" to check over. An occupation of this kind was more suitable to the determined younger sister than the quiet widow.

In crazy Montana even her determination was accepted as seemly. Her mixture of customs, starvation for lack of books combined with open hunting for a fellow pilgrim on this earthly plain, which went on without help of mother or chaperone,—this did not cause amusement. The resolute huntress was in reality a respectable enough person,—that is for Helena. She had no tact, nor the warmth, serenity or noble pride of her older sister, but the latter was an exceptional person, while she was but an ordinary town-dweller of settled western family. And she was better off that way, as she could be happy even in Montana, listening to the boasts and dissertations on various kinds of lead from the lips of the metallurgist, who, speaking parenthetically, found in this sister the only one in our company who would listen attentively to his words. Her patience in this regard I attribute to innate goodness of heart, a virtue she shared with her sister and the three daughters, with all, in fact, of the members of this secluded family. And so I took a liking to this determined aunt, hunting for a good catch in Montana.

With such an over-abundance of women in the house, I did not take it amiss that every evening the bachelors of Helena appeared there, coming to court in full costumes of western fashion, in high boots, in new silk belts, gawdy flannels or beautifully embroidered jackets made of elk hide, and snow-white trousers with back pockets from which the handles of revolvers fashioned of silver modestly peeped. They sat on the veranda, forming a whole row of figures, all silent and all chewing prime tobacco, casting long glances at the door. It turned out that one of the bolder of these, after a month of such visits, would get up his courage to go into the house, to address one of the maidens, and ask her to go walking in the moonlight. A refusal meant that the visits of this particular young blade were not looked upon with favor. Acceptance would mean the beginning of a flirtation, that in the West is the prelude to a romance.

Our young ladies always gave a negative answer. They all wanted to go back to Minnesota with their mother, but the aunt had her own ideas. In spite of the determination of that row of silent suitors, not one of the porch-sitters got anywhere. There wasn't an evening when I could see a single unoccupied chair, and some sat on the floor. The places of those who had got the brushoff were taken at once by others, coming to try their luck.

The invasion did not make the widow angry, as she knew people and their needs. Each and every one of the callers was waiting with longing in his heart for an opportunity to gaze upon a rosy cheek and to hear the swish of feminine garments. In addition to the aunt, the house contained three maidens, the oldest somewhat above nineteen, the youngest, as she boasted, but sixteen.

In the West women marry young, so that even the youngest of the three, though seemingly but a child in years, had married contemporaries. I learned all this not long after being admitted a member of the "club of elite."

I also heard more: in fact I heard that the name of Langenor was being passed from lip to lip. The telegraph operator whispered to me once that our hostess had less objection to my friend than to the other bachelors. The year before, when Langenor also had belonged to the chosen ones, everyone was of the opinion that he was in fact looked upon with favor there. It was even rumored that the widow herself would relax her principles for him, so as not to leave any daughter in Montana. When Langenor went hunting, she was obviously worried about his success. Evenings around the fireplace she regaled her daughters with his virtues. When he was at home, she always managed to direct things so that he remained in the dining room alone with Miss Matilda. The kerosene lamp was turned low. Matilda took her time gathering up the plates. But the trapper never broke the silence, or if he did break it, spoke only of the weather and beavers.

So the mother tried her luck with Susanna. Once she even asked him to escort this second daughter to church, claiming she had a headache and the other two girls were occupied with the housework. The misanthrope took upon himself this Sunday excursion and carried it out to the satisfaction of the whole family. Three days later the whole town was sure that the squatter was going after Susie. Langenor heard the rumor and so took it to heart that he stopped going to the widow's at all, sending the little redskin devil three times a day to bring him his meals.

This year, who knows, he might be accused of attacking Salomea, who from her fifteenth year had belonged to the ranks of "bachelors' enemy." What then, after he had withdrawn from the temple of the Three Graces? Perhaps he heard of the dangerous aunt!

She understood the situation perfectly. Lacking the classic features of Matilda, the freshness of Susie, and the naive charm of fifteen year old Salomea, she had to use to the full her one asset: determination. She had come to Helena to speculate in matrimony, and if she could but capture Langenor, the catch would be a good one.

CHAPTER EIGHT

Woman Trouble: White and Red

Before the aunt began her campaign, there took place a scene which was to have an important and decisive effect on the future of my sojourn here. The little redskin devil (we never called our silent boy by any other name) vanished one day. Langenor was out in the field without any dinner.

The solicitous widow wanted to send him his meal by the youngest daughter, but the aunt offered to perform this service, saying that the young girl ought not to expose herself to the danger she would be in, among all those cattle. I pointed out to them both that Texas cattle are as dangerous to aunts as to nieces. They go wild at sight of a bit of colored cloth or a person to whom they are not accustomed. Even the sight of someone walking quietly along can rouse these cattle. It would be hard for anyone to go among them without endangering his life.

And so it was decided that I myself should be the one to carry Langenor his meal. I hastened out on the prairie with an eye cocked for danger from that mass of cattle. The oxen were scattered all over the pasture, lying about and chewing their cuds, so I dared venture among them. Langenor's mustang, saddled and tied with a long lasso, was grazing near a boulder, one of those errant masses of granite, brought from God knows where at the time of the deluge or in the ice age and flung about the valleys in the form of chapels and dwelling houses.

As befitted a Montanan, I was wearing soft foot-gear, those comfortable, soft, attractive, mocassins made of elkskin, sewn and decorated with beads and straw, the work of patient Indian fingers. Such shoes do not make the slightest sound in the grass, and so I went silently, like a snake, right up to the boulder behind which the shepherd was resting.

As I approached the rock, I could hear a voice, pleasant, but powerful, worthy of the chief of a brigade, and familiar to me. I wondered with whom Langenor was talking out there in the wilderness. No one replied to the voice I had heard. Was my always so practical friend stricken with Hamlet's disease, and carrying on a soliloquy with himself? I was about to cough, to warn him that someone was listening, as I do not like to overhear a confession. Then a sound hit my ear that sent a tremor through my whole body, like an electric shock. I found myself unable to speak. I stood there, rooted to the ground.

For Langenor was declaiming from memory, or perhaps reading, obviously in order to practice speaking a tongue long unused. That he was unaccustomed to the tongue was clear from his pronunciation of some of the consonants, also the way he accented, and a certain strange singing of the words. He was speaking slowly, with feeling:

> O Niemen, my native river, where are the waters
> That once I dipped with infant hands,
> On which in later years I swam to lonely wild,
> Seeking to cool a restless heart?

Here Laura....[33]

He stopped. I understood the singing manner of his accent. And so we were not only fellow-countrymen, but the same province had borne us both. Though he read a sonnet to the River Niemen, he did not sing the words as the Lithuanian does. Other oddities of pronunciation told me that he had not heard a fellow-countryman for a long, long time. His *ś* he pronounced like *sz*, his *l* and *ł* were not true Polish sounds, but influenced by the English *l*, that half-tone so difficult to imitate.

Langenor sighed. I heard a slight sound, like the turning of a page. Then he closed the little book...and repeated from memory:

> O Dniester, my native river, where are your springs,
> And with them so much happiness, such hope?
> Where is the country merrymaking of those childhood
>   years?
>
> Where the more sweet unease of turbulent age?
> Where is my Laura?[34]

Again he sighed, and without finishing the verse murmured under his breath, "Where is she, my Laura? Does she remember? Does she too remember?"

He was silent. The silence was so great that I could hear the clatter and clink of the mustang. Slowly, step by step, I withdrew from where I had stood. Having got a distance away, I coughed, and then right away struck the tin box in which I was carrying his dinner and went back again to the boulder. Langenor stood up. He was putting a small green-bound book in his coat. From a fleeting glance I could see that its corners were worn. He hid the little volume as if it were a holy relic that for years and years he had carried about with him so as to read, when he was alone, the language which he avoided in converstion.

I displayed the mask of an actor, who sometimes has to control with iron will every movement of the muscles of his face, painting his cheeks red with berries, feigning tears, pretending he does not understand what his ears have heard, lest he arouse apprehension.

I left Langenor his meal and returned to town.

I still lived with Langenor under a single roof for a long time and ate from the same plate, but I never once told him that I had uncovered part at least of his secret. He had given me his confidence, and I was too proud to break his trust in me. But I made up my mind, nevertheless, that I would not rest until I had found that small green book. Langenor did not always take it with him when he went to the field. And so, as I expected, on the first white page of the little volume I found the rest of his secret. His name was one already known to me, and one without a blemish, though renowned for eccentricity. I had stolen his secret, to be sure, but at once I made a vow that I would never betray it without a good reason.

The very same day of my great discovery out on the prairie, Aunt Esther surprised us all.

Langenor returned to his stockade, driving his cattle ahead of him. He had to cross a street leading to Helena among neglected mine-shafts. The slovenly town, whose houses more often than not consisted of old tin, bags, and discarded papers, rather than of proper boards, occupied the space once full of gold, and was dug up with trenches, caves, furrowed with mine-shafts, so that it looked like an enormous sieve. Anyone wishing to build had to level the ground and fill it with stones and waste of every kind, torn from the bosom of the earth by the miners and left on its surface. Among these caves and heaps of stone a month never went by without some accident happening. People broke their legs on the uneven ground, horses fell into the caves and mine-shafts.

The street mentioned above had been levelled at the expense of the town to a width of a dozen or more feet. They had flanked it with a pyramid of stones built from the street up in a kind of wall, so that they wouldn't roll down on the road. Wild raspberries and thistles had grown up in the chinks of this wall, covering the stones with their branches, which were now barren of leaves.

Langenor drove his herd along, the oxen taking their own good time, picking their way and pausing to crop the tufts of grass in the road, with the unhurried greediness of cattle that you always notice when they are going toward the stable. For two hours before this they hadn't shown any interest in cropping the good grass of the pasture, but now they were greedy for the dusty thistles wherever they cropped up along the road.

Langenor sat bent over in his saddle, head bowed, and, as he later confessed, thinking of the unhappy position of one who had to replace a housekeeper with that little red devil who just at dinner time took off and would have left his boss without anything to eat all day if he hadn't had a good friend.

Just at this moment a cry rang out.

"Danger! Save me!"

Langenor awoke from his dreaming and looked ahead of him. On the highest stone of the wall beside the roadway, he beheld an apparition. It was in the form of a woman.

Apparently she had taken refuge there without regard to the raspberries and thistles, out of fear of Langenor's cattle. Burdock burrs had fastened themselves all over her dress, having, as everybody knows, a particular affinity for women's clothes. A white cap that shadowed the eyes, similar to the kind worn by sisters of mercy, veiled her face. She had fastened it with a checkered kerchief, so that the wind would not carry it away. A gray dress, pulled up for walking, revealed a shapely little leg, although one obviously belonging to a countrywoman and built not only for looks but for walking. The lady's imprudent gown betrayed even the edge of a white stocking... And when she turned her head around so that the jealous cap did not veil her face, lucky Langenor beheld features fair indeed.

The woman's hands were waving about like the wings of a windmill. In one she held a parasol, in the other a handkerchief. With these frightful weapons and a voice full of terror, she threatened the cattle, which beset her citadel, shook their immense Texan horns, like those of Hungarian cattle, and pawed the earth with their hoofs, menacing in their own way the human figure outlined against the evening sky.

Langenor did not delay the rescue. He drove the cattle away from the spot, got down from his horse, and offered the lady help. She supported herself on his shoulders, then jumped down with the grace of a gazelle. But then she stumbled... Langenor grabbed her in his arms, so that she wouldn't fall. Unfortunately, he lost his balance as he tried to save her, and the two of them tumbled together into a hawthorn bush and faded nettles at the foot of the wall. Common suffering eased the formality of their first meeting.

For a minute the two sat there together by the road, she murmuring words of gratitude, he trying to get rid of burdock burrs. Finally he managed to get to his feet, lift her up and apologize for the way his cattle had behaved. The poor creature cried...why, this was the only street that would take her home and she had been trying to go along it...and not only the squatter's cattle were roving about here. Today's adventure had taught her never to go walking along outside the limits of Helena. The squatter took a look at his cattle. Oxen and mustangs were making their way to the stable, that pale-face friend and the little red devil had closed the stockade. Langenor forced himself to a resolute deed. He took the lady by the arm and led her home, under the fire of eyes and tongues belonging to all the hangers-on who were at their usual game of dice on the veranda in front of the pharmacy, the favorite gathering place of the local good-for-nothings.

On returning to his cabin, what did Langenor find but a young Indian maiden. The Indian boy had brought his wife! He had married her "till death," this very day. This was too much even for Langenor, long-suffering as he was, and he preceded a cross-questioning of the young pair by a bath, a new experience for them. From the lips of the lad's beloved he later learned that she herself was but twelve years old,—her husband was sixteen. A family we knew had brought her up and even sent her to school. She was the only Indian girl in Helena, and except for Langenor's boy there were no redskins in the town. Their common race and the natural drawing together of two of similar color had set the two hearts on fire. They had fallen in love, she had run away from her guardians, and taken refuge under the roof that sheltered her lover. And that formality constituted the whole of their marriage ceremony.

"Thunder and lightning on them all!" Langenor cried, as he listened to the confession. "Didn't I have enough trouble with that red devil before. Now I'll take charge of this thing myself. I know the Indian! Once having tasted the sweetness of love, they won't stay apart, you'll see. I'll take the girl back to her guardians, naturally, but I know that he will fly right back to her and she to him. God's punishment, for sure!"

My friend was silent, then added after a little, as if speaking to himself, "It'.1 be hard to go on living this way any longer. I could have seen long ago that it would turn out this way. An Indian lad his age will either run away to the wilderness or bring home a wife. Even if he stayed with me and didn't take a wife, I couldn't put up with this lazy-bones any longer...and this disorder."

As a matter of fact, the cabin did not present a very pleasant sight. The table was covered with dirty utensils, the floor hadn't been swept for at least three days.

"Oh well, I'll have to look for a cure while there's still time," Langenor groaned, then fell into silence.

CHAPTER NINE

Odyssey's End

And Langenor meant what he said. He reformed completely, at once. I noticed that he took from the bag on his packsaddle a clean jacket, handsomely decorated. He bought a hat of the newest fashion in Montana, with wings as big as a parasol. In the shadow of these wings he looked more handsome than usual. His manly stature and intelligent features would have conquered the most stubborn little heart in Helena, though he was more than thirty years old, even if he had not possessed that reputation for bravery and not been regarded as one of the best and most settled individuals in ten counties.

He began now to take his meals in our circle of the elite and even would sometimes sit there all day long. Miss Esther had never before taken the place of her industrious sister and nieces, but now she shared with them the cares of the establishment. It was pleasant to watch her little hand fluttering in and out among the glistening utensils. It is true her little paws were rough,... so much the better. Langenor was looking for rough little paws, to be sure. The change in Langenor's appearance spoiled the metallurgist's good-nature, and soured the younger misses. The widow also betrayed dissatisfaction. Apparently she couldn't sacrifice the loss of a permanent son-in-law even for the possibility of a good brother-in-law. The three daughters sometimes giggled maliciously. Langenor looked at times as if he wished in his soul that the earth would swallow him up. He never betrayed by a word, however, that he was forced to the visits which sometimes lasted until a late hour, or that the walks hand in hand which always led them through an empty, familiar street, ever gave him anything but pleasure.

Only once did he speak to me on the matter of marriage, and this happened when I had taken occasion to praise the widow and her daughters, compliments which were called forth by a better than ordinary Sunday dinner.

"They all of them aim to be good workers," Langenor murmured, with accent on the "all."

"But this is an exceptional family," he went on. "It's too bad the daughters don't have the chance to meet a better class of women than you find here in Montana. But they have time for that. The young ones...they'll be leaving here in the spring."

"As soon as that?" I asked in surprise.

"Hm..that is, if the aunt would come to an agreement with her sister for the purchase of a home, they could leave. It would be better for her and for the girls as well. Even the oldest of them needs some wider vision, experience. Some fellow of good judgment, looking not only for a pretty little face and a plump figure, could take into his home such a shy little goose."

"Her mother would not share your opinion," I cried, with a sneer. "And she herself regards her education as finished."

"I know that... some of the young miners, not yet dry behind their ears, think the same and would give their gold for that pleasing little number. But anyone who's got the sentiment knocked out of his head and some sense in it, who wants to settle down, won't marry a girl considerably younger than himself and of childish manners.

I understood what Langenor was trying to say and conceded he was right.

A few days later, in the midst of a bitter winter, I took leave of Montana, for the east, for the world of cities, noise, luxury, and sights. I had to go, although doing so exposed me to the deadly tempests of the limitless plains separating Montana from other parts of the country. I took leave of Langenor, saying farewell for a long time, perhaps forever. As we parted, I expressed satisfaction that he had given up hunting in the winter in the forest and with obvious success was trapping a doe, which for him, to tell the truth, would be a more suitable companion than the Comanche princess or the romantic modiste.

He bowed his head and whispered, "Common sense has d spelled the phantom of the past. I have to choose to live in a very narrow circle and it seems to me I'll be making the best choice that way...if I make the decision and stick to it."

A month later I was riding in a sleigh about the streets of Chicago, those streets so full of life, crowded with a series of five-story palaces, as if the horror of the fire had never destroyed half that city. I could hardly believe I was riding in the midst of a section burned to ashes only a few years before.

The rest of the winter I spent among my fellow-countrymen, where I was greeted in the morning with a merry "Good morning," at a table with Polish dishes and papers in my own language from the evening before.

Whoever, reading papers published a thousand miles from his homeland, has not had his eyes fill with tears at the fourth page of these papers? It is the most interesting page of all, reminding you forcefully who the readers are who peruse these papers every day.

As we turn the third page, often certain words meet our eye, words repeated several times with slight changes each time in names and dates. The words go like this:

> Wife (mother, father, brother or other relative), inconsolable with longing, seeks Mr. N. N., who left (here follows the name of the town, city, or county) at the age of 18 for America. His last letter was sent from X., 6 years ago. Since then there has been no word. If one of his relatives in America has known the above-mentioned N. N., or has word of the day of his death and the place, and would give this word to the editor of this paper, he would be rewarded with the undying gratitude of the one signing below.

Never before had I been able to answer one of those brief notices, so moving to us, that seek to find lost individuals who may be wandering among foreigners, forgetful of distant friends and of the most holy ties. I always read all notices of this kind, hopeful that the accident of seeing them will enable me to fulfill the greatest service that is within the power of a human being to perform: to bring together people who love each other and have been separated.

The fields were already growing green, though the leaves were not yet out on the trees in the parks and along the streets, when I read an appeal of this sort. Only in this case the one seeking was not a mother or father but a friend, an attorney looking for one who had vanished nineteen years ago and was presumed to have gone to the United States. He had not been heard from in all that time. The article stated that if the lost one would write to the one whose name accompanied the appeal, he would learn something of value and importance to himself. Whoever should happen to know of the place of the lost one's residence, or death, and would inform the nearest Consul of a certain monarchy of this, would in due time receive from his family (or his heirs) proper reward for his trouble.

Need I add that the name of the one sought was the one I had read on the first page of that little green book in Helena?

I sat right down at my desk and packed up the paper and mailed it to K. Langenor in Helena City, Montana. Not satisfied with this, I wrote a few words to the attorney mentioned in the appeal, since he happened to be a friend of mine, who had helped me in the past with various money matters. I told him that if the foolishness of the hermit forbade me to let his whereabouts be known to his relatives, they could settle the matter as they saw fit. I had learned his secret without using any cunning tricks and was not under obligation to guard it under the circumstances, and it seemed to me that in the light of the appeal in the paper it was not right for me to keep silent. In order that Langenor might be fully aware of from whom the newspaper came, I wrote my address clearly on the outside of the package.

Three months went by. Summer heat like that of the Egyptian desert had already driven the people of Chicago from the asphalt wastes, hotter than the Sahara. Whoever was able, had fled the city and its burning streets, and I myself was getting ready to go to a cooler location, amid pine trees fragrant with the balsam of resin flowing in the form of amber pearls from flexible branches, to a part of the country shaded by webs with their eternally green needles, and reflecting rows of slender fir trees in blue Lake Superior.

And then I received an unexpected letter. From the careless and warped script in which it was written, I knew whom it was from. For I had seen that handwriting before, a year before, on the white page of that small green volume in Helena. That handwriting had revealed to me the true name of K. Langenor.

The letter was written in Polish, and read as follows:

Helena City, Montana
August 1, 18..

Dear Fellow-Wanderer,

Among the dispensations of Divine Providence inscrutable to me in the past, have always been—newspapers and journalists. What purpose do they serve, I have thought? Even Montana grasshoppers are good for something: they make excellent food for trout. But journalists? Those creatures who, without knowing how to conduct their own affairs, interfere in the affairs of the whole world... And yet, thanks to the fourth page of a newspaper received from you, I have to admit that the appeal found there makes up somewhat for the harm done to mankind by the other sections of newspapers.

Not wishing to bore you with a long drawn out story of the outcome of your finding the appeal, let me say at once that I revealed myself to the attorney mentioned in the paper and even before I could get an answer to my letter, he sent me directly a tearful letter with news of relatives and friends, with questions as to how I am getting along and what I have been doing all these long years. He must have received my address from you. I can guess where you learned my real name.

If you had ever asked me directly who I was, I would have told you, but when I had failed to confess our common national origin on first meeting...ah, so many of those you meet here use that entering wedge to build up great pretensions!... Later I was ashamed of my mistake and stubbornly kept silent. It was wrong for me to do this. Forgive me. Your guess has rebuked me properly. I beg your pardon for sins of so many years standing, and trust they will be given indulgence.

My friend wrote me in regard to estate matters. As usual with us, the estate to which I was heir was mortgaged almost to the extent of its full value, but the attorney thought that by putting in capital and by dint of hard work it could be saved from the hands of intriguers.

The letter from him reached me when I had already retired to the canyon, to which I went as spring came on, in order to prepare to move to Helena and settle in the city permanently. Before receiving the letter, I learned something of great importance, which changed my situation. Man proposes, but God disposes, and when you left me those books to amuse myself with, you never expected any results to come from my evening reading.

The way I was educated, we were taught a variety of things, almost all of which I have forgotten, since I never expected to use anything I had learned in my lifetime. They taught me something about astronomy...but until I fell in love with the stars of the wilderness, I couldn't identify even the most important constellations. I remembered the titles of the categories of Linnaeus, and the leafless, one-leafed and two-leafed types of Candolle, but I couldn't give the names of our own less common plants, to say nothing of describing their use. Words like "orichtognosia" were familiar to me, but I couldn't assess the lumps of metal that I found. In the West I learned to recognize gold-bearing soil and the more common silver ore, that brought me more profit than school mineralogy had done.

From the books you left for me I learned more. On returning home I learned to recognize the metal zinc, of which uncounted veins cut through my own claim. The black sand taken from a stream where I was looking for gold turned out to contain 50 per cent zinc. When I collected on the hills silver-bearing quartz, I stumbled over zinc, I built the foundation of my house of zinc, dug trenches through zinc, and the cascade which, in your words, had a metallic sound as it struck, actually proved to ring with metal. Those Holy Cross Mountains that so enchanted you, in their crowns of the morning sun, their hoods of blue glaciers, coifed with nets of mist and threads of water flowing down, shaking with braids of fir trees, contain more zinc in their granite bosoms than Cornwall ever produced in the days of the Phoenicians. Perhaps you can appreciate my delight. I have never gone after easy profit, but still I was not angered by this turn of good luck that of its own free will fate had so lavishly poured into my hand from the abundance of that rocky corner.

My delight was the more heartfelt in that I now could offer more than a squatter's cabin to the one whom, on returning to Helena, I expected to make my lifetime companion. I had put off a formal proposal... memories of the past still plagued me. I had put off setting the exact day when I would return, but we had an understanding, and I did not have any doubt that she would answer in the affirmative once I proposed. But the whole affair had cooled. The marvelous change in my fortune did not change my chances,—of that I was sure, but only added lustre to my charms in her eyes. Women of the West like a "good catch."

You know I would give a whole mountain of zinc for portraits of several of those women, from the Comanche princess to the last of my acquaintances. I would have a collection of types of the women of this strange country, who know so well how to count the worth of their charms and are so well-advised on how to exploit them in the wilderness.

That letter from across the sea ended with a signature, and like all signatures, those final words contained more news than all the rest of the letter put together. My friend sent me greetings from — Anusia.

And not just Anusia, but "Miss Anusia."

Well, what did that mean, and who was "Miss Anusia?"

To the miracles of modern civilization I count the fact that so tiny a hole as Helena, Montana, was linked by telegraph wires with another, no better known corner of the world, by which I mean T. in P[odolia]. Can you imagine how my mustang raced from the stockade to Helena, when I write that before a week had passed I learned why she was still "Miss Anusia." Always the same old story...repentance too late... finally parting.

You must remember that she never supposed that I was leaving for good, and so she kept waiting for me to return. Resigned to her fate, yet hoping, the way a woman does when her heart is broken. And I? Have mercy on me...never thinking, never looking back, never writing, thinking only of Comanches and Cheyennes.

I would have left Helena long ago, but a company has been formed here to exploit my discoveries. Believing that a bird in the hand is worth two in the bush, and wanting to return home, I sold my rights to this company and now I have more idle gold than I had ever looked upon in my wildest dreams. Now I can leave.

Here, no one will shed a tear for me. A successor has already dried the tears of the only one who might weep, and whom I myself promoted, with proper caution. He is none other than the metallurgist, now president of the great company of united miners and smelters in Helena.

It turned out that I hurt his case, not without her help, as he was looking after her, but that incident on the wall turned her attention to me. I have now made full restitution, in giving the prize back to him. He regards this service as evidence of my graciousness. He says that he has always contended that Montana would be found loaded with zinc, and that it was due to his learning that I went into the mountains and began looking for the metal according to his specifications. All in Helena believe him and I don't say them nay, and so they chose him president of the company.

I am surprised at myself, that after so many years of never taking up a pen I have managed to write this long letter. O, sweet Polish tongue! To forget you is not seemly!

If your affairs permit, wait for me in Chicago. In a week I'll clasp you by the hand in our Polish way, and if our non-western custom of kissing does not affront you, I'll do that too, in our fashion. I want to assure you, also, that however justly you accused me of timidity, lack of tact, etc., in certain matters, I aim to correct these failings. I have muffed several valuable opportunities, but if she to whom I am returning will not take me back, it will not be the fault of your grateful and affectionate

Langenor

NOTES

1. *Koronacja Krola Wysp Fidzi* 1953 ed., 252-53.

2. *Dzieci Krolowej Oceanii*, 1956 ed., 87, cited on p. 470 of an article on Wisniowski in *Obraz literatury polskiej XIX i XX wieku*, Instytut badan literackich Polskiej Akademji Nauk, Warsaw, 1966, Vol. II. This was kindly made available to us by Dr. R. Krystyna Dietrich.

3. Henryk Sienkiewicz (1846-1916), at the time of his visit to the United States in 1876 a young journalist with none of the works by which he is today known abroad to his credit.

4. Most of the letters of Sienkiewicz referred to by Wisniowski were printed in serial form in the Warsaw *Gazeta Polska*, where they appeared intermittently between 1876 and 1878. Other letters appeared in other journals during this period, one, finally, as late as 1879. Wisniowski's words on Sienkiewicz were printed in the journal *Wedrowiec* No. 38, 1877. By the time he wrote this assessment of his fellow-countryman, Wisniowski had undoubtedly read the early letters, which began appearing on May 9, 1876.

5. "Praised be...," first words of the greeting commonly exchanged by devout Poles.

6. City in India, famous for diamonds and other treasures.

7. John Baptist Purcell, consecrated as bishop, Oct. 13, 1833; archbishop, July 19, 1850; died July 4, 1883. He was the second bishop and first archbishop of Cincinnati.

8. A reference to *A Voyage to Icaria*, by Etienne Cabet, published in Paris in French in 1840 and in English in 1845. Inspired by More's *Utopia*, Cabet actually tried to establish an ideal community, which he called Icaria, on the Red River in Texas. The community was unsuccessful from the start, and in 1864 was dissolved.

9. The brothers Remak were Gustave (1827-86), a lawyer; Stanley, an officer in the U. S. Army; and Stephen S., a lawyer (1831-90), for a time American Consul at Trieste.

10. There was never a deliberate **Kulturkampf** (Culture War) against the Roman Catholic Church on a scale comparable to Bismarck's. Despite the popular prejudice against a third term, it is true that, not so much Grant himself, but certain managers of the Republican party, did attempt to secure Grant's nomination, following his retirement in 1877. Despite the popular prejudice against a third term, it is true that, not so much Grant himself, but certain managers of the Republican party, did attempt to secure Grant's nomination, following his retirement in 1877.

11. The Reverend John Pitass (1844-1913). Born in Niemieckie Piekary, Upper Silesia, Pitass came to the United States in 1873 and settled in Buffalo. He was ordained there on June 7, 1873, and appointed pastor of St. Stanislaw's Church the same day. In 1874 he founded the first Polish schools in Buffalo.

12. One of the finest figures in the early history of the Polish emigration in the United States. Born in Poland, Oct. 13, 1837, Kiolbassa first became a teacher in Panna Maria, Texas, to which his family migrated. Later made a fine career in public life in Chicago, where he he was known as "Honest Pete." Died June 23, 1905. See, Helen

Busyn, "Peter Kiolbassa, Maker of Polish America," *Polish American Studies*, VIII, 3-4, July-Dec., 1951, 65-84.

13. *Gazeta Polska*, founded in 1873 by Wladyslaw Dyniewicz. It continued publishing until 1913.

14. We have not been able to identify this paper.

15. *The Pilgrim (Pielgrzym)* was founded in Union, Missouri, by Jan Barzynski, brother of the Reverend Wincenty Barzynski, for whom see Note 16, below. The first number appeared on March 29, 1872. The paper was later moved to Chicago, not Detroit, where the first number of the new series appeared Sept. 15, 1874.

16. One of the most distinguished of the Chicago priests was the Reverend Adolph Bakanowski, C. R., who arrived from Texas in 1870 and became pastor of St. Stanislaus Kostka Church. It is probable Wisniowski met him just before he left for Rome. The most distinguished of Chicago's Polish priests was, of course, the Reverend Wincenty Barzynski, also a member of the Resurrectionist Order. Barzynski also came up from Texas, in 1872, as assistant to Father Bakanowski, whom he succeeded as pastor in 1874, and remained in this office until his death on May 2, 1899. He was one of the greatest organizers of Polish life in the history of the Polish people in this country. For both Bakanowski and Barzynski, see *Polish Circuit Rider*, a translation by M. M. Coleman of the Texas memoirs of Bakanowski, Cherry Hill Books, 1971.

17. For a history of the Polish communities in Texas, see Jacek Przygoda, *Texas Pioneers from Poland*, Waco, Texas, 1971: also Stefan Nesterowicz, *Travel Notes*, translated by M. M. Coleman, Cherry Hill Books, 1970, and the Bakanowski memoir cited in Note 16.

18. Captain Jack, as he was called by the Americans, was the leader of the Modoc Indians of Oregon and California in 1873 when the tribe attempted to reoccupy lands ceded by them under pressure to the United States.

19. New Ulm, a city eighty-eight miles southwest of Minneapolis, on the southwest bank of the Minnesota River, also on the Cottonwood River, which here enters the Minnesota. Founded in 1854 by the German American Land Association of Chicago and laid out with wide streets and parks. The region was Sioux territory, and in 1862 members of this tribe attacked the town. The settlers fled to Mankato, down the Minnesota River, but later returned to complete the town they had begun.

20. A morg is 1.38 acres.

21. Omitted here are two pages describing in detail the operations of the railroad promoters.

22. The great panic of 1873, touched off by the failure on Sept. 18 of Jay Cooke and Company, one of the leading banking houses in the United States. The failure was caused by over-building of railroads in the west.

23. Wisniowski's little farm must have been in the vicinity of Springfield, on the Cottonwood River, west of New Ulm, as we find a reference in the *New Ulm Herald* of July 1, 1874 to his having to leave Springfield because of the grasshoppers. This reference was received from Mrs. Leota M. Kellett, Director of the Historical Museum of Brown County, New Ulm, Minnesota, July 30, 1971.

24. Thomas Brassey (1805-70), English railway contractor. Besides building railways all over England and later in France, Holland, Belgium, etc., he also built the one from Lwow to Czernowitz, as Wisniowski says. Later he was to operate in Asia, America, and Australia.

25. The Anti-Monopolist parties arose in the years 1873-76 in the Midwest and parts of the Far West as an agrarian movement calling for government reforms similar to those advocated by the Granger Movement. These organizations disappeared after the national election of 1876.

26. A favorite Polish dish, made of beef.

27. Here Wisniowski goes into a long description of the Fox and Wisconsin Rivers. He took a sailboat trip down the Wisconsin. The country fascinated him, both the landscape and its history, and he imagined the ghost of Hiawatha was about. At the sound of the falls of Hiawatha, he says, he dreamed of a project that would hold back the tide of mad colonization of this wonderful country, which he saw as already robbed of any feeling for its original inhabitants. But for such a project he lacked the force of will necessary to carry it through.

28. "The hut how blest, that shares with guest."

29. This magnificent formation is best seen on the road from Leadville, Colorado, to Grand Junction. It was hardly known at all before 1869 and was not named until several years later. Longfellow's poem, "The Cross of Snow," and the paintings of Thomas Moran, made the unique formation known to the world. Lines from Longfellow's poem could well have been used by Wisniowski, instead of those from Heine, as the "motto" of *Langenor*:

> There is a mountain in the distant West
>   That, sun-defying, in its deep ravines,
> Displays a across of snow upon its side.
> Such is the cross I wear upon my breast,
>   These eighteen years, through all the changing scenes
> And seasons, changeless since the day she died.

30. Salomon Gessner (1730-88), Swiss idyllic poet, landscape painter, and engraver.

31. On the night of August 6th, 1857, the Cheyennes made their most lurid attack on the Union Pacific railroad of that year. It took place near Plum Creek, 59 miles east of North Platte. No emigrant train was involved, as in Langenor's story, but employees of the railroad were massacred. See Wesley S. Griswold, *A Work of Giants*, pp. 220-21.

32. Augustina Zaragoza, the Maid of Saragossa, distinguished for her heroism when the town was besieged in 1808 and 1809, and celebrated by Byron in *Childe Harold*, Canto I, liv-lvi.

33. The lines are from the first stanza of the sonnet "Do Niemna," To the Niemen, by the poet Adam Mickiewicz (1798-1855).

34. Langenor has here composed his own poem to the river of his particular homeland, basing it on Mickiewicz's sonnet to his native stream. The theme of reawakening of Polishness through the poetry of Mickiewicz, as exemplified here in *Langenor*, anticipates Sienkiewicz's story, often translated, *Latarnik*, The Lighthouse-keeper, published in 1882. *Langenor* appeared in *Kurier Warszawski*, in 1877.